D0874289

HOW TO BUILD A FORTUNE
INVESTING IN LAND

HOW TO BUILD A FORTUNE
INVESTING IN LAND

John E. Kirk

Prentice-Hall, Inc., Englewood Cliffs, N.J.

To Vivienne, Michael and Dennis

Prentice-Hall International, Inc., *London*
Prentice-Hall of Australia, Pty. Ltd., *Sydney*
Prentice-Hall of Canada, Ltd., *Toronto*
Prentice-Hall of India Private Ltd., *New Delphi*
Prentice-Hall of Japan, Inc., *Tokyo*

© 1973 by
Prentice-Hall, Inc.
Englewood Cliffs, N.J.

*All rights reserved. No part of this book
may be reproduced in any form or by any
means, without permission in writing from
the publisher.*

This publication is designed to provide accurate and
authoritative information in regard to the subject matter
covered. It is sold with the understanding that the publisher is not engaged in rendering legal, accounting, or
other professional service. If legal advice or other expert
assistance is required, the services of a competent professional person should be sought.

. . .From a Declaration of Principles jointly adopted
by a Committee of American Bar Association and a
Committee of Publishers and Associations.

Library of Congress Cataloging in Publication Data

Kirk, John E
    How to build a fortune investing in land.

    1. Real estate investment.   I.   Title.
HD1395.K57   332.6'324   73-985
ISBN 0-13-402982-8

Printed in the United States of America

A Word from the Author

After years of answering thousands of questions about making money in land, I decided that a book on the subject was urgently needed. At first I was reluctant to write such a book. After all, individuals and corporations had paid me thousands of dollars to answer their questions on land investments. Why then should I take the time to write a book that would answer all these questions and would sell for only a few dollars?

Because of my personal experiences and my close association with other successful land investors, I felt that I was uniquely qualified to author such a book. The obvious need and perhaps my own ego were too powerful, so here is my book, *How to Build a Fortune Investing in Land.* It has been designed to be complete and detailed, yet easy to read and, more important, easy to understand. To my knowledge there is no other single source of so much factual information on how to profit from land investments.

Here in one volume you can learn: How land investments pay hundreds and even thousands percent profits. How to make big profits in land and never invest one dollar of your own money. Why land is considered the safest of all investments. How to *buy* the right land at the right price on the right terms, and then how and when to sell all or part of it for big profits. How to reduce the income tax on these profits. How Mr. R. R. retired to his favorite fishing spot and has $25,000 a year for life from one land

5

investment . How a 23-year-old man fresh out of college has made thousands of dollars from land while serving in the Marine Corps. How a man who bought the cheapest, worst farm, by using one of the methods explained in this book, made $127,000 from a total investment of only $5,000. These are only a few of the tested money-making, fortune-building plans, methods and ideas contained in this book.

Considering all the information this book contains, it is in fact a complete "course" in investing for profits in land. In your hand you have the facts and figures that you can use to invest and make money in land. Wealth and financial security come from the land more than from any other source.

Now you can get your share of that wealth. I hope that the information in this book will bring you the happiness and sense of achievement it has brought me.

John E. Kirk

ACKNOWLEDGMENT

Many of the ads in this book have appeared in the following publications:

The Des Moines Register and Tribune, The Joplin Globe, The Kansas City Kansan, Kansas City Star, Omaha World Herald, St. Louis Post-Dispatch, Springfield News-Leader & Press, Topeka Capital-State Journal, Tulsa World and Tribune, TV Guide, Wichita Eagle-Beacon.

Contents

9

How to Borrow Your Way to a Real Estate Fortune (*continued*)

The Nonnegotiator 56. Special Financial Footnote 56. $200,000 from $5,000 56. Buy Land by Contract with No Cash 57. They Didn't Know the System 57. Call in an Expert 57. New Sales Plan Gets Action 58. Use the Seller's Credit 64. You Recommend the Plan 65. You Show the Way 65. Examples of Profits from Buying Right 65. Cash Makes a Profit 65. Terms Make the Deal Possible 66. No Cash Deals 66. Buying Right Guarantees Profit 66.

Options Defined 68. Legal Points 69. Reasons for Options 69. Ordinary Options in Use 69. Special Options 70. Advantages to the Buyer 71. No Cash Options 71. The No Option, Option 72. I Had Everything but the Money 72. The Verbal Option 73. Most People Keep Their Word 73. How to Profit from a Verbal Option 73. Profit for All 74. Profit from Land You Never Buy 74. Sell the Option 74. Who Buys the Option 74. Sell the Plan, Not the Land 75. Why Sell the Option 75. You Can Profit from Options If 75. Bad Deal Avoided by Use of an Option 76. A $1,000 Option Gets 10 Percent of a Million Dollars 76.

Zoning Defined 78. Zoning Recap 79. Who Controls Zoning 79. Times Change 80. Zoning Can Be Changed 80. How to Apply for a Zoning Change 82. Council Refuses Office Zoning 82. Attend Zoning Hearings 82. Making Your Application 83. Review of Procedure 83. Use of Law, Logic, and Persuasion 83. Keep Your Cool 84. Prove and Persuade 84. No Can Change to Yes 85. Appeals for Justice 85. Zoning as a Land Investment Tool 85. Zoned Commercial Makes Profits 86. Buy Where Zoning Should Change 86. Know Zoning Before You Buy 87. A Final Look at Zoning 87. Mr. B Zones Himself a Fortune 87.

Why, What, and Consequences 89. How to Find Trading Opportunities 90. Best Source 90. Word of Mouth 91. Trading Land for Land 91. No Cash Needed 92. Trades for Goods and Services 94. Reduces Need for Cash 94. Trading Helps Sales 94. Co-Ownership 95. Regular Co-Ownership 95. Perfect for Spare Time Dealer 96. Once More from the Top 96. Special Note on Brokers 97. Special Tax Notice 97. Young Lawyer Makes $80,000 in Land 97. Old Lawyer Retires 97. Co-Ownership and a Trade Makes Everybody Happy 98.

Exhibits

1

The Fabulous Money-Making Opportunities in Land

It is a fact that many people have and are making their *fortune in land.* These people are doing this as their only business or while holding down other jobs, operating completely unrelated businesses, or practicing a profession. Full time, part time, any time is the right time to make your *fortune in land.*

Land investors come from every walk of life, every educational and social background. All are making money from land; some are making their *fortune.*

A WONDERFUL THING ABOUT LAND

The amazing and wonderful thing about dealing in land is that it is available without discrimination. It is available to all who will learn and apply certain proven methods. These *proven profit principles* are explained in detail in this book.

ONE THOUSAND PERCENT PROFIT?

For perhaps the first time in your life you will know how profits of hundreds and thousands percent are made in land deals.

You will learn the exact procedures that can be applied by you to duplicate these fortune-building land investments.

SUPER PERFECT PROFIT MAKER

The nature of land is passive. This inherent passive nature is the key that makes land the super-perfect profit-making investment. Land as an investment offers the highest return in relation to the time and money invested. Because land is passive, it can be put aside when your employment, business, or profession demands your full attention. It can be put aside in confidence that the passage of time, plus inflation and population explosion, will add to its value.

THE TURN ON, TURN OFF INVESTMENT

Here is an investment you can turn on and off as you wish. You can devote just the amount of time that you have available. You can invest the amount of time that you wish to give to increasing your income and your net worth. You decide to turn it on small or you can turn it on in a big way. You can, if you wish, turn on a fortune. You can be in the land business at any level you choose.

YES, IT REALLY IS THAT EASY

Land is not subject to theft, it doesn't deteriorate, and it doesn't need constant attention. In fact you can, if you use the buying principles outlined in this book, buy land, pay the small annual taxes, and literally forget you own it. In time, without any effort, you will be able to sell this land at a profit, and quite possibly at a very large profit.

Land investments can be as easy as *buy, hold, sell,* and *profit.* It can be the profitable investment that takes almost no time, very little money, yet still yields substantial profits.

ADD WORK TO ADD PROFITS

In general, you can best profit in land by putting your time to work, creating through your actions added values and profits. How to do this is explained many times with many actual examples in subsequent chapters in this book. How you can become an active investor; how you can reap monetary rewards for your efforts; all of this is explained in detail.

Yes, you will find that land is indeed the perfect fortune-making investment.

OPEN TO YOU

The best thing about the opportunities for profit and possibly a *fortune in land* is this fact: *This Opportunity Is Open to You.*

INCOME NOW

I recommend that you generally deal in land on a medium-to long-range program. If, however, you need cash now, if you need income now, land can do it.

You will learn in this book how to buy land for immediate resale at a profit. You will learn how to find the proper land, how to negotiate, how to buy or obtain control of the land you want. Then you will learn numerous ways to sell the land immediately and at a profit. You will also learn how to obtain all cash or how to sell on terms and have an income for years.

NOW IS THE TIME

If you want an income and you want it now, read this book now. Then reread the sections that tell you how to profit now. Follow the *profit principles* and *proven methods* that can be like a road map to those profits.

If you will devote at least a part of your time to one of these land projects, *you* will wake up one morning and have that income you want. It will take effort and it will take desire, but it can be done—and the methods are in your hand.

TAX-FREE FORTUNE BUILDING

The author of this book believes that the great advantage of land as a fortune builder is in its ability to build net worth without creating tax liability. In simple terms, your estate grows in value, yet you do not have to pay large amounts of income taxes. In fact, you may have a tax deduction.

This is accomplished by your purchasing land that will increase in value. You are not taxed on this increase in value. You pay no taxes until you sell all or part of the land and actually receive the cash profits from this increase. *Special note:* The real estate tax you pay on this property is a tax deductible item.

AN EXAMPLE

You purchase 40 acres of land located in the path of urban growth. Cost to you—$400 per acre. You hold this land for ten years; value after ten years—$1,250 per acre. Your estate is now worth $50,000 and you have had an increase in net worth of $34,000. Your only cost has been the annual real estate taxes and, as previously noted, these were tax deductible.

You are now worth $34,000 more and you owe no income tax on this increase in your estate. You now have a number of options.

1. Sell the entire tract for cash, and pay income tax on the profits. If this is your only land transaction, you can probably qualify for long-term capital gains.

2. Sell part of the tract each year and pay taxes on the profits from each part as it is sold. This, depending on your other personal income, would reduce the total tax, as you would not be in a high tax bracket in one given year.

3. Sell the land or parts of the land on terms. Take payments spread over a number of years. If you conform to the proper tax regulations, you can spread your income and substantially reduce your tax liability.

4. You can hold this land until your personal income is very low. This applies especially to sale of land after you retire: then you can sell on any of the above bases. You can have income for years with a very low tax cost. Be sure to consult your lawyer for applicable tax regulations.

Remember, as long as you do not sell your land holdings you will have no income tax liability. Your land and consequently your worth may increase in value many times. As long as you do not convert to cash or equivalent income, there is no tax on the increase.

1,000 PERCENT VALUE INCREASE, NO TAX

The author has land that has increased in value ten times in as many years. Yet until this land is sold and that increase received in cash, no tax liability has been incurred. The estate is increased, so now—

YOU CAN BORROW CASH ON TAX-FREE INCREASE

The increase in value of a piece of land is a tangible asset. It can be appraised and money can be obtained from lenders using the appraised value as collateral.

Using our previous example as a base: the land cost $16,000, the increase in value was $34,000, the appraised value of the land is $50,000. It would be possible to borrow at least $25,000 on this property. There would be no income tax liability on this $25,000, and in addition the interest payments would be tax deductible.

You can build a fortune in land and not pay income taxes on this fortune. You may even have certain tax deductions to help reduce your tax on your regular income.

FORTUNE BUILDING AT ITS BEST

Now we come to the no cash profit principle. Let's repeat: the *no cash profit principle.*

If you have heard the saying, "It takes money to make money," don't you believe it. You can deal and profit in land without any cash investment. You will learn in this book many ways to buy and control land without a down payment. You can, for example, become a partner with the owner of land. You can obtain 100 percent financing from many sources; this is accepted practice in dealing in land, to minimize the cash investment. This is the profit principle of—

MONEY LEVERAGE

This is the principle that turns your knowledge into money; the principle that makes one dollar do the work of a hundred. This leverage is an everyday tool in the land investment business.

You can contract for and control large or small parcels of land without one dime of your money being involved. You can sell all or part of this land and pay for it out of its own income, and make a profit.

LAND INCOME PAYS FOR THE LAND, PLUS A PROFIT

Yes, the income from the land pays for the land and gives you a profit. The examples of profitable no cash land deals are so many that it would be impossible to cover them all. Many such "no cash" deals are explained in detail in this book.

CASH IS AN ADVANTAGE

Even though it is common practice to deal in land on a small or no cash basis, it is generally better if you have a reservoir of investment and operational cash. It is, however, definitely not a requirement.

YOU CAN DO IT

You can, using the methods in this book coupled with your efforts, make money in land with or without cash. The time needed to start you on the road to a fortune in land may be less time than many persons devote to golf or bowling.

SPARE TIME OR FULL TIME

Spare time is defined differently by different people. You may consider any time you are not working at your regular occupation as your spare time. Another person may include his work time, plus time for his family or his hobby as time he would not be able to devote to a side venture. Some people have more than one spare time method of increasing their earnings or their estate.

You are the only judge of what is your spare time. You must evaluate your personal life, your occupation, your family, and then decide how much time you wish to consider your spare time.

IT'S YOUR SPARE TIME. SPEND IT, WASTE IT, INVEST IT?

Land is the perfect spare time investment, because it can be tailored to your personal spare time situation. As I have pointed out earlier, you can invest and profit in land using almost none of your time. It is also a fact that as you increase the amount of time you devote to your land deals, the better the chances for larger profits.

The amount of time many persons spend on the golf course can easily be sufficient for a moderate to large land investment program. If making a fortune is worth that amount of time to you, then land could be the investment opportunity you are looking for.

BE A FULL TIME DEALER-INVESTOR

The full time dealer-investor in land can and does reap the largest profits. Being able to research, test, buy and sell on a full time basis will expedite the process of profit-making in land. Land dealing and investing is an interesting and exciting way to make money. It can and does make it possible for a person to travel, meet interesting people while living the good life, with much of the cost a tax deductible item.

You can, if you wish, become a full time investor-dealer in land. Whether you decide to spend part time or full time investing in land, such investments can and will make you a fortune.

LIFETIME FINANCIAL SECURITY

It's bad enough to be poor when you are young. To be poor in one's old age is a tragedy. Visualize being old and dependent on others. Couple old age with poor health and very little money.

That would most surely be an unhappy time for all concerned. How, then, in a world of high prices, higher taxes, and rampant inflation, can anyone achieve financial security?

LAND CAN BE THE ANSWER

Land can answer both the what and the how of the financial security question. Most people cannot afford to make large payments on annuity-type insurance policies. Most people cannot take large amounts of money out of present income to risk on investments in the stock market. Very few people can risk quitting their regular job to go into business for themselves.

The above factors force many people to live their entire lives spending their income and hoping that things will work out in the future. Hope without effort and planning generally leads to heartbreak and disappointment. To have worked all your life and then find that inflation, taxes, and the high cost of living have left you very little to soothe the path of later years is sad indeed.

YES, YOU CAN DO IT

Now you have available to you what has been for many the answer to this dilemma. You can solve this financial problem if you will do the following:

1. Put into practice the *profit principles* and methods in this book.
2. Determine now that this is what you want to do.
3. Persevere.

If you use care, if you work at it, you can build financial security for you and your family.

Yes, you can build a *fortune in land,* and this book can make it possible.

ACTUAL CASE HISTORIES

Now read about real land deals that have made profits and fortunes for others.

Mr. B. Listens and Profits. Mr. B. makes a profit from listening and then doing. Mr. B. had been one of four partners in a resort land deal that had not been profitable. Mr. B. and his partners were forced to give half the income from their land to a land dealer who had the know-how to profitably develop and sell their land.

Mr. B. observed, listened and learned from the methods used by the land dealer. Mr. B. asked questions and listened to the answers. Then Mr. B. acted.

Mr. B. purchased his own resort acreage. Using the methods he had learned from the dealer in land, Mr. B. executed a development and sales plan that was very successful. Mr. B. then sold his operation to a large real estate development company at a substantial profit and retired to Florida a wealthy man.

This is a true story. I know it is true because the author of this book was the land dealer who, without knowing he was doing so, taught Mr. B. the land development business. Here is an example of the benefits of watching, listening, and learning. Mr. B. profited from the knowledge that the author had gained the hard way. Mr. B. took the same short cut you can take. The methods used by Mr. B. to make his fortune are all in this book. Do as Mr. B. did—apply them. They may well make your fortune, too.

Mr. K. Uses His Real Estate Agent. Mr. K. is a 23-year-old college student. Mr. K. does not have family wealth, yet at age twenty-three he owns a substantial amount of land, much of it paid for.

How could this very young man, while attending college, deal profitably in land? The answer is that Mr. K. put into effect a well-conceived land-dealing plan. Mr. K's plan was actually based on his own *lack* of experience and his *lack* of knowledge in the real estate field.

Mr. K. profited, the real estate broker profited, and, surprising as it may seem, the buyers of Mr. K's land profited by being able to buy small tracts or lots that fit their needs and desires.

Everyone is happy and Mr. K., at 23 years of age, is well on his way to his fortune as a dealer in land. Yes, this again is a true story. Mr. K. is now serving as an officer in the United State Marine Corps and was the roommate of the author's son at Quantico, Virginia.

I have recommended that Mr. K. and my son expand into more and bigger land deals. I believe in land as a fortune maker enough to want my sons to become dealers in land.

Mr. K. decided to use the knowledge, experience, and desire for profit that is basic in most professional real estate brokers.

Mr. K. watched the advertising of real estate brokers in the area of his choice. Using a chart system, he determined that one specific broker was very successful at making repeated sales of the same properties at ever-increasing prices. With this knowledge, Mr. K. made an appointment with his selected real estate broker.

Mr. K. explained that he wanted to buy some land as an investment. He admitted he would have to be able to buy the land with a very small down payment. Mr. K. also told the broker that he would not only buy land through this broker, but would also let this same broker represent him in the sale of his land.

The broker was already very much aware that two commissions were better than one. He was also a man who could recognize a young man who might be developed into a continuing source of business. It was a fortunate meeting for both parties.

Starting with a few acres and only a few hundred dollars as a down payment, he resold at a profit, using his original money plus the profit to buy more land. Mr. K. repeated this process during his college years and was on his way to his fortune in land.

2

How to Turn a Few Dollars into a Fortune in Land

Land. The good Lord only made so much of it, then quit. He didn't, however, quit making people, so we have the population explosion. We have more and more need for land, with only the original amount available.

The above fact of life has created the greatest money-making opportunity that any generation has ever seen. You can't say, "If I had been born twenty years sooner or later I could have made my fortune." The time is now; the opportunity is now. It is up to the individual to take advantage of this natural chain of events.

PROOF OF PROFITS IN LAND

This book will prove that it is literally impossible to lose money dealing in land. Note, I said land, not houses, apartments, offices, commercial buildings—not any type of construction. I am talking about land and land only.

Production ceased in the land-making business when God rested on the seventh day. Then Adam and Eve started the chain reaction that has never stopped—and begot—and begot—and on and on. The greatest natural force in existence makes the land shortage become more acute each year. Now add the second great ingredient to this product—rampant inflation. Now the balloon soars up, up, and

away. Static supply, population explosion, rampant inflation—
these three put together have created the greatest money-making
opportunity in the history of the world.

There is actually a fortune waiting for anyone—I repeat—anyone
who will invest all or part of his time in land.

The best news about this opportunity in land is that it is
available to almost any economic level. Any person can participate. In later chapters, you will learn how it is possible to profit
from land with no investment of money. Other times, with only a
few hundred dollars you can make thousands. No, not dreams, but
reality. It's being done every day—being done right now by
ordinary people, using simple, basic rules, using their heads,
exerting a little or a lot of energy. Your friends talk about an
investment return of 6 and 10 percent. Land can return 100, 500,
1,000 percent—again, not fancies, these are easily proven facts—
land is the great investment for any person and can be participated
in at any level.

A FEW DOLLARS TO A FORTUNE

Land investments can be pyramided: first a few dollars, then a
few hundred, then thousands, then hundreds of thousands; land
does not perish; it cannot be carried away by thieves; it cannot be
vandalized; it requires no maintenance; you don't have to heat or
cool it. It is the passive investment. Time is on your team; land,
almost without exception, becomes more valuable merely by the
passage of time. Time plus inflation means you can profit by
sitting on the sidelines. Add some special circumstances, a highway, population shift; add a lake, industry, or recreation, and your
land can boom overnight.

ALMOST ALL GREAT WEALTH THROUGH LAND

When considering land as an investment, remember that the
basis for all the great wealth in the world has always been real
estate. Trace the background of almost any wealthy family and
you will find that land played a great part in the acquiring of that
family wealth.

The most important factor about land as the road to riches is that any normally intelligent person can make money in land. A very intelligent person can make a fortune.

The author of this book most certainly does not have an I.Q. above normal. Yet he has been able to make thousands of dollars and build an estate in excess of a quarter of a million dollars by dealing in land, and at the same time have a regular full time job. In other words, land—full time or as a sideline—can be a pleasure and a profit. The only question is your desire.

This book will tell you how. This book is based on the author's experiences and on experiences of others. It will give you a complete course in how you can build your own fortune in land.

THE SYSTEM STEP BY STEP

To prepare you for the chapters to follow, I will cover the main points of the system of dealing profitably in land. I will give you the outline of the areas that will be covered in detail in these chapters.

> Chapter Three "When, Where, and Why to Buy Land Profitably"— *Where . When . Why* of land buying covers a wide area . *Where* can be determined by where you are . Where do you want to be . Also, what is around the land . roads . highways . towns . cities . country . lakes . shopping centers . offices . schools . churches . hospitals . recreational, etc . Learning the *where* is a major step in land profits . Now the *when* . spring . summer . fall . winter . No two pieces of land are alike . No two locations are the same . *When* to buy . The seller decides for you . The price decides . The terms decide . Your needs decide for you . Your customers decide . Any time may be the right time . When you know the right facts . The *when* decision will be made for you . Here you are learning how to get the facts. The *Why* is based on the fact that when opportunity knocks you buy because it is a good profit opportunity. When you have that special deal offered to you, then it becomes more why not than why. Knowing *where, when* and *why* to buy land is indeed the foundation of your *fortune in land*

Chapter Four may well be the most important chapter in this book.

> Chapter Four is titled, "How to Borrow Your Way to a Real Estate Fortune"—If profits are the children of sales, then buying right is the

father . When you buy the right land at the right price on the right terms, profit is automatic . Buying the right land at the right time on the right terms takes knowledge, study and careful planning . However, it is not difficult if you know the *system* . Even buying without cash is only the application of certain basic and logical principles . It can be done . Yes, you can buy land without any cash investment . You can use your credit . Or the seller's credit. You can get all types of financing . 100 percent loans . 110 percent plus loans . Interest-free loans . And many, many more . Read the examples of profits from buying right . Learn the art of buying the right land on the right terms, and you are more than half way to your fortune in land

In any business there are what can be referred to as tricks of the trade. They are not actually tricks; they are knowledge that is not known to the general public.

Such information is contained in Chapter Five, "Options and How to Use Them to Your Advantage;" learn the least known method of dealing in land with little or no capital . The spare time dealer in land can test and practice dealing in land virtually without risk through the use of options . Here are the answers . What is an option . When to use an option . What are the various types of options . Finally, options in use in actual profitable land deals

Chapter Six, "Zoning, Your Key to Big Profit"—Change the zoning to make a profit . What is zoning . Why have zoning laws . Who controls zoning . How can the land dealer get zoning changed or amended . Procedures . Legal aids . Logic of need for change . Politics . Persuasion . Appeal for change based on injustice of present zoning . A simple change from zoned residential to zoned commercial can change a $2,000 residential lot into a $25,000 commercial building site . Zoning and how to get it changed can be a key element in the system for making a fortune in land

Chapter Seven is based on one of man's oldest instincts.

Chapter Seven covers "Trades and Co-Ownership Partners in Profit."—"Every man a horse trader" is in the oldest of American traditions . In acquiring land and in developing land, we can use this no cash method of barter and exchange to make phenomenal profits . Here is a way to increase your assets and your future earnings without incurring tax liabilities . Trade land for land . Trade land for goods .

Trade land for services and all at a profit . Trade your way to co-ownership . Buy your way to co-ownership . Co-ownership is in some cases the best arrangement for the dealer in land

Chapter Eight, "Secrets of Legal Tax Avoidance"—They say a man who is his own lawyer has a fool for a client . Chapter Eight tells you how to obtain the best legal aid at lowest cost . It shows you how to help your lawyer help you . It gives you legal and tax information that lets you keep more of your profits . This chapter gives you the peace of mind that comes from knowing how to avoid legal and tax problems . Why two lawyers . When to use your customer's lawyer and why . Tips on legal ways to conserve the estate you are building with your land program

Here is the chapter that will pay for this book hundreds of times.

Chapter Nine, "Protecting Your Profits with the Right Documents"—Information plus samples of various documents and forms used to buy, sell, option and exchange land . A ready reference of the usual and the unusual forms . Some of these documents and forms make buying and selling land easy and automatic . The dealer in land will find this chapter a much needed reservoir of sample forms and information as to their use

Chapter Ten is titled "Sell Some—Hold Some—Fortune-Building Technique"—The magic profit formula . Chapter Ten covers the greatest, easiest method of legally making money I have ever known . This is the method that allows you to buy, sell, and keep your land, all with one piece of property . Buy, sell, hold, I repeat, buy, sell, hold . This may sound like a contradiction . How can you at one and the same time sell and hold a piece of property . One of the oldest methods of dealing profitably in land . It lends itself to the land dealer like no other system . You can take profits or increase your assets almost at will . Learn how you can own many pieces of property without ever having a large amount of your money invested . And without a large debt . Read actual "Sell Some—Hold Some" deals that combine immediate profit with substantial increases in land holdings for the future . This technique can lead the land dealer to a position of financial security only dreamed of by most people

Chapter Eleven, "Effective Psychology That Sells Land"—This chapter will teach you what may be the most effective psychological sales system ever used . Once you become the person applying this profit principle, the doors to almost unlimited profitable sales will open . Here you can take advantage of selling to the magical mass market . This chapter will tell you how your prospective customer feels, thinks, and what he wants . With this knowledge you supply his desires . His needs . And when you have done this, the sale is made . Apply this psychological profit principle to land and your fortune in land is only a matter of time

CREDIT A WAY OF LIFE AND A WAY TO PROFIT

Chapter Twelve, "Buy Now–Pay Later for Fast Profits in Land"–Is in effect a course in the use of credit . You, the land dealer, will use credit to obtain control of land, to make improvements on this land . Then you will apply the profit principle of credit to the sale of your land . People are acclimated to purchasing on some form of time payment plan. They accept the time payment interest charge

As Chapter Twelve points out, the buyers are in many cases more interested in the amount they pay per month than in the total amount they are paying for the property.

TWO PROFITS ON ONE SALE

Here we find two areas of profit, first the profit on the land, second the profit from the percentage charged for selling on terms. The greatest benefit to be derived from selling land on terms is the making of more sales to more people, plus the fact that you can sell to lower income groups. I don't need to tell the reader that there are more people in the middle and lower income bracket. More prospects, more sales, more profits.

Almost everyone uses credit to buy . Now, you can use credit selling to increase your income and your total wealth . You sell on credit . You make more sales . You increase your profit . You, through credit selling, can establish an income for years and years to come . Credit selling is the great sales maker . Credit selling spreads your income and makes it legally possible for you to pay less income tax . You can make your fortune selling land on credit

Chapter Thirteen, "How to Create Value and Put Money in Your Pocket"–Shows you how your actions . Your efforts can creat *profits in land* . Profits that will exceed your fondest dreams . You can change a low-cost piece of land into a desirable, easy to sell, high-priced piece of property . Learn the many ways you can *create value* . Yes, you can become the *action person* . The profits are where the *action* is. Believe in this action *profit principle* and you can change a dull, unused piece of land into a moving, action-packed, almost living thing. This action principle makes land prices grow like grass in the spring

This action principle is one of the most important forces in life. Read Chapter Thirteen more than once; it could change your life.

Chapter Fourteen, "Mail Order Selling: Money in Your Mailbox"— This is without a doubt the perfect way to sell land . You can do it at home . Use your evenings . Your weekends . Let the mailman work for you . The thrill of opening your mail and counting the money must be experienced to be appreciated . Learn how to select the right land . The letters, forms and systems to use . Then practice with tested, proven advertising and advertising techniques . See and read samples of all the various ads . Special materials and methods of follow-up that create sales . How to resell previous buyers, their friends and relatives . Case histories of successful selling of land by mail . Tested details of how the author and others have sold hundreds of thousands of dollars worth of land by mail . Methods you can duplicate in your own home

Chapter Fifteen, "Advertising and Sales Promotions that Really Produce for You"—You pay for it or get it free . Advertising is the life blood of selling . Learn when, where and how to advertise . See samples of the best advertising material . Learn the basics of advertising that sells land . Discover *word of mouth advertising,* it's *free* . Your customers can be your best sales force . Don't forget your friends, relatives and business associates as a source of sales promotion assistance at no cost . Deliver a good product at a fair price . Keep your word . Treat people fairly . Your reputation is either advertising for or against you . Next is example after example of advertising and sales promotions that have sold and are still selling land at a profit . And at your finger tips a collection of sample advertising and sales promotion material

START YOUR LAND FORTUNE NOW

Chapter Sixteen "Tested Fortune Making Programs"—Is the chapter that shows you step by step how to start making your fortune with your first land deal . Now, a bigger deal . Again, step by step, to more profits . Practice, knowledge, and effort will make it possible for you to go *big deal* . Yes, you can really make a fortune dealing in land.

You have in your hands a complete course in investing, dealing and making money from land. *Read this book carefully, then decide to make your fortune in land.*

SPECIAL NOTE

The material in this book is based on actual experiences and in many cases on specific land transactions. Circumstances may vary from time to time and place to place. The author cannot guarantee that any method or procedure outlined in this book, if followed by the reader, will result in a profitable business venture.

The author can only say that all of the methods and procedures in this book have been used in the past with profitable results. Many of these methods and procedures are being used profitably at the present time by the author and thousands of other people.

As the legal requirements regarding land transactions change from time to time, always check with competent legal counsel prior to buying, trading, or selling land. Sample forms, contracts, deeds, advertisements, etc., that are found in this book may become obsolete and may not conform to current laws and regulations. This material should not be copied or used without checking with your lawyer as to its legality.

3

When, Where, and Why
to Buy Land Profitably

It is very important that the dealer in land be able to answer these three questions.

1. *Where* to buy land?
2. *When* to buy land?
3. *Why* buy land?

The answers to these questions are part of the profit principle of the system for profitably dealing in land. This chapter will give you the answers to these questions.

1. WHERE TO BUY LAND

Where you should buy land is based on where you as an individual dealer desire to deal in land. You must select from the various areas and opportunities available. Select the area that you feel offers the best possibilities for pleasure and profit. You may find that you have a special affinity for a certain area or a certain type property. If you have or can develop such an affinity, the question of where you should deal in land will be very easy for you to answer.

Specialize

It is easier, and generally speaking it will give you more pleasure and profit, to deal in a specific type of property. It is difficult for the land dealer to be an expert in all areas and types of land available. The next few pages will assist you in finding your answer to the question of where you should specialize.

Urban Property?

It may seem at first glance that urban areas offer the least opportunities for dealing in land. It would appear that there is very little, if any, unimproved vacant land in the city. It is a fact that there is very little vacant and unimproved land in urban areas. Most urban property has buildings or improvements of some type. Where, then, is the opportunity for dealing in land in the city?

Urban Renewal

The biggest governmental program in our nation's history will be the rebuilding of our cities. More programs and more money than you and I can conceive will be part of this urban renewal. The city, county, state and federal governments will all be deeply involved.

You will see whole areas of old buildings, old apartments and old homes bulldozed out of existence. In a matter of weeks, acres and acres of land will be brought back to its original state. Profitable land opportunities will be in abundance in every city.

Know the Programs

Buying city land for profit will require your learning about all the different government programs. Then, by buying run-down properties in selected areas, properties that you know will fit one or more of these urban redevelopment programs, you will be in the path of progress, and progress means profits to the land dealer. If you do your homework well, these programs will come to the land you have purchased.

Financing the Key

You will be able to resell such urban property with relative ease because financing will be easy. The government programs have government-backed or -sponsored loans. These loans are easier to get and in general carry lower than normal interest rates.

The people who build apartments, office buildings and factories as a business will be your willing and able buyers. If you use knowledge and care in your urban property selection, its resale at a profit will be assured.

Take a Look at the City

Don't overlook the field of urban development and the land profit opportunities it offers. If you live in or near a medium or large city, take a good look at what may be to you the old home town. Right in your own area may be your golden opportunity.

You may feel you already know the area. Don't let your preconceived and many times erroneous notions hold you back. Take a fresh look; take a look based on knowledge of what the future holds. Look with new eyes; see what is really going on. Talk to bankers, lawyers and businessmen. Ask them about the future of your city. Ask them what is happening and what they feel will happen. These men are generally only too happy to talk of the city's future. Remember, their success is tied to the future of the city.

Next, talk to the Small Business Administration. Get the pamphlets covering the government programs already in existence. Ask them to keep you informed as new programs are put into effect. You will find that the governmental agencies of today are staffed by intelligent and helpful people. Your tax dollars pay for these agencies; use them.

Watch all news media, contact your local senator, keep on top of all new urban renewal legislation proposed or passed. Remember, urban renewal may well be the biggest boom in land and land values of this century. Ask yourself if this is the area of operation for you as a dealer in land. It could be that your land fortune is in your own home town.

Suburban Property

Here is the area that appears to be a better opportunity than it really is. Because the suburbs are and have been the boom areas, it seems everyone thinks of the suburbs as the land investment gold mine. The very fact that the suburbs have been and are booming makes profitable land investments difficult to find. The dealer in land profits most by dealing in areas that are not being developed at the time of his purchase.

If you do decide to try your land-dealing hand in the suburbs, here are a few tips. Be very careful; act only after checking and double checking. You are playing in a game where experts are dealing. The suburbs are the operating area of the biggest monied, top real estate men in the business. These are the full time professionals.

Most of the vacant land in the suburbs is in strong ownership. When I say suburbs, I mean many miles out from the center city. In these outlying areas, well-financed speculators have control over large acreages. They are engaged in doing the same thing you want to do—they are holding for growth and development.

Opportunities for the Prudent

After reading the foregoing, you may feel that you should forget the suburbs. The truth is that there are many profitable land opportunities in the suburbs. Because it is an active area, you can, if you are diligent and careful, locate some "sleeper" deals that the professionals have overlooked.

The pros, as a general rule, are not interested in small pieces of land. Check your suburbs for small, unimproved lots or tracts of land. Check the records—find out who owns each piece of vacant land. If possible, contact the owners indirectly. By indirectly, I mean try not to appear interested in the purchase of the land.

By this method, you may be able to find out why the owner hasn't sold or won't sell the property. It may be that he doesn't want to sell; maybe he can't sell. It is also possible that you will find the owner will sell if approached in the right manner. Sometimes an owner will sell to an individual when he will not sell to a real estate company or a big name developer. You are out to develop those contacts if you want to buy right.

Convert to Profit

You may, through this process, find a profitable land opportunity in the suburbs. In many cases, the best way to profit from a single lot or a small tract of land is to create a use. You must increase the value of the property by developing a new or better use. Here is where you create a use and then sell and profit from the increased value created by this use. The possible uses for any piece of land in the suburbs may be many. In subsequent chapters you will learn the methods used to create and sell new and better land use.

The Suburbs May Be for You

You are trying to decide whether to deal in land in the suburbs. The answer can only be obtained by looking your suburban opportunities over very carefully. Check out the potential profit properties, obtain prices, terms, etc. You may be able to obtain an option on one or more of these pieces of land.

You can then see if you can put into effect the created use sales method. Through the use of an option you can test market without a large monetary risk.

Zoning: a Key to Profit

The suburbs offer some excellent profit opportunities to the dealer in land who can get the best zoning for a piece of land. It is easy to imagine the difference in the value of a lot zoned for a single family dwelling and the same lot zoned for an apartment. When considering the suburbs, zoning can be all-important in determining the value of property. (See Chapter Six.)

Financing Can Be a Plus in the Suburbs

One big advantage the land in the suburbs has over almost any other land—it is, in general, very easy to finance. The market for land in the suburbs is active. Most lending institutions consider good land in the suburbs excellent collateral.

You may find that the money leverage created by this easier financing will help you decide whether you should pick the suburbs as the place to start making your fortune in land.

Country Property

Where does the suburbs end and the country begin? With factories, office buildings, hospitals, shopping centers, etc., being built around the outer perimeter of the suburbs, we now find we must be forty, fifty, or sixty miles or more from the core city before we are in the country.

With the modern automobile, superhighways and turnpikes, a fifty-mile drive takes only forty-five minutes. As an example, a person having a job with one of the industries or business firms located on the outer edge of the suburbs can live in the country, yet be closer to his place of employment than the person who lives in the downtown area of the city.

Escape: A Key to Profit

Most people originally moved from the city to the suburbs for two reasons: one, to escape high city taxes; two, to get away from the congestion, noise and crowded conditions of the city. Look at our suburbs today, jammed with two, even three-car families. Shopping centers with their parking lots packed with cars, families trying to get from their car to the store areas without being run over by families in cars coming in or going out of the parking area. It's Russian roulette with automobiles in the suburbs.

With the building of more schools, plus streets, sewers, etc., the taxes for the suburban home owner are unbelievable, and in some cases unbearable. Add these things up and you find the same pressures that created the suburbs are starting a chain reaction that is creating a new living area for many people. That new living area is the area we now call the country.

Best, Easiest Land Profits

I am certain of one fact. The "in close" country property offers the best, easiest and cheapest area for the dealer in land to operate. Here is the area that you can spend the least time, the smallest amount of money, and end up making a fortune.

The How to Do Method

The method for converting the country around you into your personal fortune will be found in detail in this book. You will find examples, suggestion, ideas, and actual step-by-step methods.

You can select country property as your area of operation with the sure knowledge that this is where you can practice dealing in land with the least risk. All the natural factors to keep you out of trouble are already present in land located in the country. Remember, we are speaking primarily of country properties located near medium or large centers of population. Never was the time better or the opportunity more immediate. Country land is the prime fortune-building opportunity.

Resort Property

Resort property is the author's personal favorite area to deal in land. It is to me the fun area of land development. It brings you into contact with more people, and with these people when they are in a vacation, retirement, pleasure frame of mind. Your customer buys more with his heart than his head. In resort property you are selling a dream.

Make Dreams Come True and Profit

You are the person that makes other people's dreams become reality. You will gain not only financial rewards; you will gain the personal satisfaction of helping people fulfill their desire for a place on the lake or the beach. You will be the supplier of someone's heart's desire, and you will do it at a profit.

Natural Beauty, A Natural for Profits

Wherever there is a lake, a river or an ocean; wherever mountains and woods create natural beauty—that is where you will find resort property. Look in the travel section of any newspaper. You will see page after page of resort areas being advertised and promoted.

Here is a fun way to get to know your product in the resort land business. Select the resort areas that appeal to you, then take short combination work and play vacations to these areas. Look; ask questions. Enjoy and learn; become the resort property expert. Then, using the lessons in this book, buy and sell at a profit the fun land of our country.

Fun and Fortune

Resort properties are a pleasure to sell if you like to sell the answer to the dreamer's dream. I can hardly conceive a better way to make your Fortune in Land.

2. WHEN TO BUY?

The answer to the "when to buy" question is simply, buy anytime you have the right land offered to you at the right price on the right terms.

There are certain times of the year when certain types of land are generally selling at their lowest prices. Resort properties, except in tropical areas, will generally be selling low in the middle of winter. In fact, December is a good month to buy any land. The reason December offers the best buys is simple—the weather conditions plus the holiday season combine to reduce the number of prospects for all land. This reduced sales activity leads to lower prices and better terms.

Bad Days Lead to Bad Buys

Be warned, even though buying land in the winter generally offers best buys, there are problems. Try not to look at land on very cold or rainy days—you will have a great tendency to not really take the time to study the land carefully. You may well be too eager to get in where it is warm or dry.

To really know your product you must examine it as carefully as possible. Weather is a factor in your examination of the land. If you rush your examination because of bad weather, you may not know your product. Not knowing your product can lead to serious error. You may buy the wrong land. For you, the dealer in land, to prosper, you must not buy the wrong land. I repeat: if at all possible, look at land on at least a moderately pleasant day. Even in the middle of winter there are good and bad days. Select those good days to look at property.

You Can't See the Land for the Leaves

When you are looking at acreage, it may have wooded areas; in the case of resort land, it may all be wooded. When the trees and brush are in full leaf, you cannot really examine wooded land.

The author was literally knocked to the ground by a deer while examining a wooded section of land. It was early fall; the brush and the trees so obstructed both my and the deer's view that we literally walked into each other. This incident illustrates an important fact relating to land selection and land development.

View land if possible when the brush and trees are leafless. Even after you have purchased the land, this leafless view can be of great importance in viewing the land relative to where to construct your roads and other improvements. You can't know the land if you can't see it.

Your Eye in the Sky

It will, of course, not be possible to look at land only under ideal conditions. The following is a land examination procedure that can be used with success almost any time of the year.

1. Get a topographical map of the land in which you are interested. (Have a land engineer explain how to interpret this type of map.)
2. Get an aerial photo of the properties. (The owner may have a topographical map and an aerial photo. The government has such photos.)
3. Drive over as much of the land as possible, and walk the balance. Take photos as you move from area to area. Use a portable tape recorder to record your observations and comments regarding the land.
4. Rent an airplane or helicopter; observe and photograph the

land from the air. (Helicopters are best; however, they are quite expensive to rent. The author uses a slow, light plane and has had very satisfactory results.)

5. Now put all your information together for study.

With this material, regardless of the time of year, you can say, "Yes, I have really examined this land;" "Yes, I know the product;" "Yes, I can buy land at any time that suits me."

You Decide the Time to Buy

Using the foregoing information, you make the time to buy coincide with your having located the right land, at the right price, on the right terms. We are back to our simple fact: if you use the method, if you know the system, ANY TIME CAN BE THE RIGHT TIME TO BUY LAND.

3. WHY BUY LAND?

If you are going to become a successful dealer in land, you will want to own or control land. The best method of controlling land starts with land ownership. This need on your part to own land is the answer to why buy land.

You can deal in other people's land. It can even be very profitable to do so. In this book, methods of doing just that are outlined. In most cases it is better and more profitable to deal in land you have either bought or are buying.

Control Is Complete

As the owner of a piece of land, you can to a great extent develop it as you please. You do not have to explain your actions. There is no committee to decide to do or not to do things. You, the owner, are in control; you make the decisions and you reap the benefits.

When you buy, you own; when you own, you control—control is one of the answers to why buy land.

More Why Buy Answers

You buy when you have an opportunity to make a profitable deal. When opportunity knocks, you buy and you profit. Seek and you shall find is a truth that applies to profit opportunities in land. When that special deal is offered to you, then it becomes more why not buy than why. The Why is control and profit—that is why you buy.

You Have the Answers

Now you can answer the Where, When, Why buy land questions. You know the answers that can and will help you make money dealing in land. Knowing WHERE, WHEN and WHY to buy land is indeed the foundation of your fortune in land.

Mr. E.T. Finds the Where, When and Why

Mr. E.T. always watched for new developments along the highways and roads as he traveled. When he sees a road or highway being rebuilt or improved, or when he sees a new group of businesses being built, he acts. Going to the County seat, he checks ownership records of ground adjacent to this new activity. He contacts these owners and generally ends up buying or getting an option to buy some of this land.

Over the years Mr. E.T. has made hundreds of land purchases on this basis. All of them have been profitable. The point to remember is stay alert. Don't drive by your fortune in land and not see it.

Mr. L.M. Asked Questions and Made His Fortune

Mr. L.M. knew the author of this book. He asked me questions; based on the answers, Mr. L.M. located land on a lake. More questions, more answers, and Mr. L.M. was in the resort property business. Mr. L.M.'s regular job was lost by him due to a change in the company's business. Mr. L.M. converted from part time to full time land dealer, and went from lake number one to lake number two, and on to his fortune from land.

The methods used by Mr. L.M. are in this book. The Where, When and Why you have just read. The How to buy and How to sell for a profit you will find in the remaining chapters. Mr. L.M. now enjoys a substantial income and financial security all from his becoming a land dealer.

Knowing Where, How and What Makes a Fortune

Mr. T. bought five acres near the edge of a large city costing $2,000. Later the land was annexed by the city. Mr. T. applied for zoning for apartments. His request was approved. With the five acres zoned for apartments, Mr. T. had plans drawn for such use. Mr. T. then sold the land, the zoning and the plans for $90,000—a profit of $88,000 minus the small taxes Mr. T. had paid while he held the land.

Here, knowing the where to buy, knowing about zoning, and knowing about creating value, all explained in detail in this book, Mr. T. put the deal together and made a veritable fortune.

4

How to Borrow Your Way to a Real Estate Fortune

For the dealer in land to profit, he must buy the right land at the right price and on the right terms. This is a fact that must never be forgotten or ignored.

PROFIT'S FATHER

The resale of land at a profit comes after the purchase of the land. If profits are the children of sales, then surely buying right is profit's father. When the right land is bought for the right price, profits are automatic.

Nothing is more important to the dealer in land than his ability to buy land on some basis that will virtually remove the financial risk. This chapter will give the methods of negotiating, contracting, and financing, along with the how of buying land for profit. You will learn the various ways you can acquire control and/or ownership of the land you want on the best basis for you.

If you studied the preceding chapter, you know *Where, When* and *Why* to buy. Now you will learn *How to buy.*

THE CASH BUYER

The cash buyer can negotiate price better than the credit or non-cash buyer. You can be the cash buyer if you have the cash;

you can also be the cash buyer without furnishing your own cash.

When you find the land that fits your plans—when the owner of this land says, "I want all cash"—you have a number of methods available to meet this all-cash demand.

We will eliminate the possibility that you already have the cash in the bank. If you do have the cash, you merely come to terms on the price and write a check. In general, it is better to conserve at least part of your cash and use one of the following methods to obtain at least a portion of the cash needed.

USE YOUR PERSONAL CREDIT

Your personal credit may be much better than you think. Take your planned and profit-projected use of the land to your banker. Take a current personal financial statement along at the same time. Explain to your banker how you intend to buy, resell and profit from the land you wish to buy. Show how you intend to repay the loan you need. Have all of this information neatly typed and in an easy to follow sequence. This will impress your banker that you know what you are doing. Gain his confidence; bank loans are made on the banker's opinion of the borrower's ability, intelligence and honesty. Collateral in many cases is not the most important reason for a bank making a loan.

Because this is your first land deal requiring a bank loan, it will probably be a small deal. Your cash requirement, therefore, will be small. Your bank may be able to supply this, your first working capital loan.

THE RELUCTANT BANK

Banks, however, are not always willing to lend money on vacant land. They are especially reluctant if the land is some distance from the bank's normal business area. As an example, if you are buying land in the country, the downtown city bank may not be willing to make the loan. Their problem is in not having anyone familiar with such property. In the event of a default on the loan, they cannot easily sell the land to recover their money.

It is important that you, the spare time dealer in land, attempt to view the situation from the standpoint of the lender. When you are making your plans, consider who would be most likely to finance land of a certain type in a certain area.

BANKERS KNOW BANKERS

Your banker may be unwilling or unable to make the loan you need, but he may be able to recommend you to another bank. This other bank may be nearer the property or may be a bank that does make loans on the type of property involved.

Banks also specialize. If you try to get a loan on land from a bank that specializes in loans to manufacturing companies or retail businesses, your chances are much less than if the bank has and does loan for land and does make loans for land development.

YOUR PERSONAL CREDIT REPUTATION

Clearly understand that getting a loan from any bank on vacant land will, in most cases, depend on your personal credit reputation. You will be using your personal credit to start your land deal. The money you obtain from the bank will make you a cash buyer as far as the land owner is concerned. Make this use of your personal credit pay off. Be sure you use this cash position to buy the land at the lowest possible price. Don't be so eager to get started that you pay more than you need to pay. Money talks, and it talks loudest in an all-cash deal. When you buy for cash, buy at the lowest price possible. Every dollar you save on the purchace price is clear profit.

CASH FROM PRIVATE SOURCES

Another method of putting yourself in the cash buyer position is to obtain money from private lenders. If buying the land with cash is the only way it can be bought, or if the cash price is substantially lower, then you can afford to pay the higher interest rates of the private lender.

Your banker, lawyer, newspaper ads, and listings in the Yellow

Pages of the phone book can put you in touch with private loan sources. Here again, your plan for the development and sale of the land plus your personal background will be the most important factors.

The private lender is generally an individual or group of individuals who have gathered together both their cash and their credit resources. In many cases, the private lender borrows the money he loans to you. He, because of his contacts and financial background, can get a better interest rate than you. He profits from what is known as the interest point spread.

> An example: The private lender borrows $10,000 at 7 percent simple interest. He loans it to you at 6 percent add on rate. The interest mathematics are as follows.
>
> Lender borrows $10,000 at 7 percent simple interest for five years, payable at $198 per month. His total interest cost for 5 (five) years is *$1,880.60.* You borrow $10,000 from this lender. You pay 6 percent add on interest. Based on 5 (five) years at $216.66 per month, total interest charged for five years is $3,000.
>
> | | |
> |---|---|
> | Private lender's interest cost | $1,880.60 |
> | Private lender's income from | |
> | interest paid by you | $3,000.00 |
> | Private lender's profit | $1,119.40 |

You may at this time ask why you should pay such a high rate of interest. We go back to the reason why you considered the private lender in the first place. The land you want can only be bought for cash, or the cash price is substantially lower than the price on terms. Also, keep in mind that if you pay the owner the higher price for the land on terms, he will also want interest on the balance.

You go to the private lender because it makes the deal possible. It may even in some cases save you money because it makes you the cash buyer. Each deal must be calculated on an individual basis. Do your money mathematics, then make the best, lowest cost deal you can.

SILENT PARTNERS

Still another method that can make you a cash land buyer is to form a partnership. This partnership should not give your partners equality in making decisions. You retain the right to handle the development and sale of the land as you think best. Your partners are what is commonly referred to as silent partners. They put up the money; they share in the profits; they do not share any responsibility in the operation of the project.

Each partner puts up a certain amount of money. For this he receives a percentage of the profits. You can even offer a lot or small parcel of land plus a percentage to each person who will put in a certain amount of money.

EXAMPLE OF A SILENT PARTNER DEAL

You are buying 100 acres of country land. Cash price for this land is $100 per acre; total price for 100 acres is $10,000. You offer to various persons one 1/2 acre lot and 10 percent interest in the profits from the resale of the entire property. They pay you $3000 for this lot and 10 percent interest. You sell 40 percent of the project to four silent partners. A partnership agreement clearly defining the entire understanding is drawn by your lawyer. This agreement is signed by you and your partners.

The 40 percent you sell brings in $12,000 cash. Here you have 120 percent financing with profit participation, instead of an interest rate as on a loan. This $12,000 pays the $10,000 for the land and leaves you with $2,000 in operating cash. Now you can put your land sales plan into operation. You follow your plan; you profit; your partners profit, and you have created a continuing profitable source of financing.

The offer of the lot as part of the deal is optional. In many cases, you will sell a percentage of the expected profits only. Be realistic in projecting your profits. Do not promise more than you can legitimately expect to deliver. Your future as a dealer in land rests on your reputation. Be honest; do your best to see that your silent partners are satisfied, and that they receive a fair return on their investment.

INCORPORATING YOUR LAND OPERATION

Using a corporate entity to buy and sell land has advantages and disadvantages. If you must raise outside capital, a small corporation may be the way you should go. With a corporation you have the advantage of limiting your personal liability in certain respects.

A corporate entity increases your bookkeeping. It also requires certain reports and tax forms to be filed with government agencies. You are under a certain amount of control and supervision by state and federal agencies.

The selling of corporate stock to raise money is controlled by state and federal laws. You must have a lawyer to guide you all the way. Decisions on the amount of stock to be issued, its par value, what price to place on the stock, when to sell, who to sell—all of these questions must be answered in consultation with your lawyer.

When you sell stock, you are selling equity; you are also getting interest-free money. Equity is ownership, so you are giving up ownership every time you sell a share in your corporation. It is easier to start a small corporate entity than it is to stop it. Don't rush into setting up a corporate structure until both you and your lawyer are sure it is needed.

START AS AN INDIVIDUAL

It is generally better to get your land operation started as an individual. After you have gained experience and success, use partners or a corporate set-up to expand. In this manner you will be using outside capital to expand, and pyramid your operations and your profits. This is one of the ways to that big fortune in land.

You have just been introduced to some ways you can buy land for cash and not use your own money. Next we will explore buying land using the seller's money.

THE SELLER FINANCES THE SALE

It is a happy fact that most land can be bought on terms with the seller carrying the mortgage. Our tax laws plus the desire of the seller to make extra profit from the interest charge makes the owners of land willing to sell on terms.

When you buy land with the owner carrying the loan you must negotiate not only the price, but you must negotiate interest rate, payment period, and in most cases a release clause arrangement as well. We will examine this method of buying land by using an example.

You find the land you want. It is 100 acres; asking price is $12,500; terms, 20 percent down, five years on the balance, interest rate 8 percent on the declining balance. You now prepare to make a counter offer. You cannot make an intelligent offer until you make a chart similar to the Buying Chart Land Project No. 1.

BUYING CHART LAND PROJECT NO. I

LOCATION *Stone* COUNTY *Missouri* STATE

TYPE OF PROPERTY *Resort* TERRAIN *wooded-hilly*

LEGAL DESCRIPTION *SEC 11-11 TWP 11 R 11, ETC.*

SPECIAL FEATURES *½ Mile Frontage on Lake*

BUILDING AND IMPROVEMENTS *Old Farmhouse*

Est. Value $750.00

ROADS IN OR FRONTING PROPERTY *Land Fronts on ¼ Mile of*

County   Black Top Road

OWNER'S REASON FOR SELLING *Retiring Farmer*

OWNER'S ATTITUDE *Friendly   Doesn't need money all at one time*

IS THERE A REAL ESTATE AGENT/if so who? *No*

MINERAL, OIL, GAS RIGHTS *All Rights Go With Property*

EXISTING MORTGAGE *No* IF SO DETAILS

EASEMENTS OR RESTRICTIONS *U.S. Govt. Lake Take Line-*

No Other

WATER SOURCE _Well (No Pump)_ ELECTRICITY _On Property_

TELEPHONE _On Property_ NAT. GAS or BUTANE _Butane_

RENTAL OR OTHER PRESENT OR FUTURE INCOME, SUCH AS HOUSE, GRAZING, WATER, MINERAL, OIL, ROCK, TIMBER, GRAVEL, FRUIT, SOD, GOV'T. CROP allotment etc. _NONE KNOWN_

NUMBER OF ACRES _100_

PLANNED USE OF LAND _Lots for week-end cottages and retirement homes._

IF SALE OF LOTS, NUMBER OF SALABLE LOTS _400_

IF TRACTS, NUMBER OF TRACTS _None_

IF BOTH, GIVE NUMBER OF EACH _____ TRACTS _____ LOTS

TAXES, BASED ON LAST YEAR _$250_

TOTAL PRICE _$12,500_ PER ACRE PRICE _$125_

PROJECTED COST FOR IMPROVEMENTS _Roads $8,000 Survey $650_ FOR ADVERTISING _$16,000_ FOR SALES COMMISSION _$24,000_ FOR ADMINISTRATIVE, TAX, INTEREST, LEGAL, AND MISC. _$15,000_ TOTAL ESTIMATED COST NOT INCLUDING LAND _$63,650_ TOTAL LAND COST _$12,500_

TOTAL ALL ESTIMATED COSTS _$76,150_

AVERAGE SALE PRICE PER LOT _$500_

TOTAL ANTICIPATED GROSS INCOME _$200,000_

ESTIMATED TOTAL PROFIT _$123,850_

ESTIMATED LENGTH OF TIME TO PREPARE FOR FIRST SALES _120 Days_

1st Year's Projected Income	$12,000
2nd " " "	20,000
3rd " " "	25,000
4th " " "	25,000
5th " " "	25,000
	$107,000

Balance to be obtained after five years _$93,000_

Cash required for payments, improvements, advt., sales, and misc. expenses

1st Year	$10,825
2nd Year	8,100
3rd Year	7,200
4th Year	7,200
5th Year	6,400
Total	$39,725

Balance to be spent after the fifth year $35,775

Cash available to use for down payment and first year costs $10,000

Based on the figures we have used in this example chart, you make the following offer.

You will pay $10,000 for the land, $1,500 down. You accept the 8 percent interest rate, but you ask for eight years to pay the balance. Point out that this extra time will mean extra interest income to the seller, plus it will reduce the income tax he pays. You ask for an acreage release clause. This clause allows you to have clear title to an acre of the land for each $200 you pay to the seller.

You will probably settle for a deal as follows.

TOTAL PRICE $11,000 (This is $1,000 more than you offered and $1,500 less than the seller asked.)

DOWN PAYMENT $2,000.00 (This is $500 more than you offered and is $500 less than seller asked.) You will probably get the additional number of years if you accept the 8 percent interest rate. If you are willing to pay in five years, you would try for a lower interest rate. The release clause may require your paying $250 for each acre released.

You can see by the foregoing both you and the seller have compromised. This is the pattern that most sales of medium to large acreage follow. This is generally not true of lot sales; it is sometimes true of sales of small tracts.

THE NONNEGOTIATOR

You may run into a seller who will not negotiate. You must then decide, based on your land purchase chart, whether to buy or not to buy. If you can't in a reasonable length of time find a better deal, if your chart indicates even at the price and terms of the seller you can make a substantial profit, then you should buy on the seller's terms.

Let the *buying chart* tell you if you should make the deal. The facts and figures should make the decision. Buy with your mind, not your heart. Buy with the facts, not your feelings. Plan, check, test, and then buy.

SPECIAL FINANCIAL FOOTNOTE

You should not need more that $5,000 in cash to put this land deal in operation. You would need the down payment, plus cash for surveying fifty lots, some road work, initial advertising, and selling costs.

As soon as you start your sales, you will create a small cash flow. This will grow larger, as your sales increase. You will be able to pay part of your first year's costs from income from sales. You should be able to pay all of your costs and show a substantial profit in your second year.

$200,000 FROM $5,000

Here $5,000 starts you in a $200,000 deal. Here is money leverage at work. Here the buyer of your lots will furnish the balance of the money needed to buy and develop the land.

This is not an unusual land deal. It may seem unusual to you, but that is only because you have never before been involved in land deals, or at least not of this type. Believe me when I tell you, deals such as this are in operation all over these United States. Full and part time land dealers using such methods are making their fortunes while you read these words.

BUY LAND BY CONTRACT WITH NO CASH

The best way to explain the no cash contract method of buying and dealing in land is to detail an actual deal. All of the following will be taken from the negotiations and completion of this actual project.

A group of men had formed a small corporation. They had purchased a 250 acre tract of land on a major government lake. They had taken title to this property through a *deed of trust*. Title was in the name of the corporation. They were using the seller as the loan source. The seller, a retired farmer, had accepted a down payment and was using a deed of trust with release arrangements as described in Chapter Ten.

THEY DIDN'T KNOW THE SYSTEM

These very successful business and professional men based their plans on their own desires. This was a major mistake. They were all either wealthy or in the upper income bracket. They spent money for an airstrip. They subdivided a portion of the land into large lots, and another part into tracts.

Their sales effort was toward their friends and business associates. They sold a number of the large lots to these people, then no sales. They ran ads, but these resulted in the sale of only a few more lots. At the end of their first year they were in the position of few sales, considerable investment, and no ideas of how to improve the situation.

CALL IN AN EXPERT

At this almost too late date, they decided to do the thing they should have done first. They decided to learn the how of dealing in land. To do this they now called in an expert. The author was a friend of one of these men. This man remembered that I was a dealer in land. He called me and we set up a meeting. All of the corporate stockholders attended.

The entire situation was discussed. They offered me 20 percent of the corporate stock if I would join them in the capacity of sales and advertising manager. I asked for time to become more familiar with the land and the problems. A short time later I accepted their offer.

NEW SALES PLAN GETS ACTION

I instituted a new plan using the following method. Part of the unplatted acreage was platted into small lots. A lot owner's park and beach area was cleared and equipped. Advertising, with terms predominant, was run in the proper newspapers.

Sales at profitable prices were made in quantity. A cash flow was developed. At this time I told the other stockholders that I would buy the entire property. I presented a plan where they would be paid out of sales income. They accepted my offer and I now took complete control of the property without putting up any money. The contractual arrangement, drawn by an experienced real estate lawyer, is shown in the Purchase Contract.

PURCHASE CONTRACT*

THIS CONTRACT IS made this _____ day of _____ , 19 __, between BLACK DEVELOPMENT CO., INC., a Missouri corporation, having its principal place of business in Kansas City, Missouri, herein called Black, and WHITE, Inc., a Missouri corporation, having its principal place of business in Kansas City, Missouri, herein called White.

In consideration of the mutual promises herein contained, IT IS AGREED:

1. Black hereby sells to White the real estate in Stone County, Missouri, described as:

(Complete detailed description of land appears here.)

---

*SPECIAL NOTE: This contract is one of the most complete agreements of its type you will ever read. It cost almost $2,000 to have this document drawn. From this single contract you can learn almost all of the fundamentals of contracting for acreage to resell as lots. This contract should only be used as a guide, and then only with competent legal assistance.

For the sum of One Hundred Fifty Thousand and 00/100 ($150,000) Dollars, payable in installments from time to time, as hereinafter provided, on or before January 1, 19___, when the then unpaid principal balance of said sum, together with all accrued and unpaid interest thereon, shall be paid in full. No interest on said sum shall accrue until January 1, 19___, after which date interest at the rate of five (5) percent per annum shall be payable on the unpaid principal balance from time to time remaining due, and said interest shall be payable annually on the first day of January of each succeeding year. If the payments made by White to Black as hereinafter provided are not sufficient to pay the interest when due, then the unpaid interest will be added to the then unpaid principal balance and bear interest at the rate of five (5) percent per annum until paid.

2. *Abstract or Title Insurance.* Within twenty (20) days from the date hereof, Black shall deliver to White abstracts of title to all of said real estate, certified from the United States Government to a date no earlier than the date of this contract, and showing merchantable fee simple title to all of said real estate to be in Black. White shall have fifteen (15) days thereafter in which to examine said abstracts of title and to submit in writing to Black any objections White may have to the condition of said title. The subject matter of said objections shall be corrected within thirty (30) days after receipt of such objections, and if not so corrected, White may elect to treat this agreement as void by notice in writing to Black following the expiration of the period granted for the correction of said objections without the same having been corrected. In lieu of furnishing such abstracts of title, or in lieu of meeting said objections, Black may cause a title guaranty insurance policy in the face amount of the subject matter of this contract to be issued by a title insurance company, authorized to insure titles in the State of Missouri, insuring White against loss by reason of unmerchantability of the title to any or all of said real estate. If Black shall elect to furnish such a title policy, a commitment therefore shall be delivered within the period initially provided as aforesaid for the furnishing of abstracts of title, or if abstracts of title shall have been furnished and Black shall thereafter elect to furnish such title insurance, the commitment therefore shall be delivered to White within the period otherwise permitted for the meeting of objections to the condition of said titles as shown by said abstracts of title.

3. *Delivery of Deed.* Contemporaneously with the execution of this agreement, Black has executed its General Warranty Deed conveying all of the real estate described as aforesaid to White, which deed has been deposited in escrow with John J. Doe subject to return to Black or delivery to White, as the case may be, as hereinafter provided.

4. *Taxes and Assessments.* Black shall pay all general and special taxes and assessments which are liens upon said real estate at the date of this contract, except that all such general, state, county and school

taxes and special assessments payable during 19____ shall be prorated over the period of said calendar year between Black and White as of the date of this contract, said proration to be payable when the title to said real estate is found acceptable as aforsaid. Thereafter White shall pay all taxes and special assessments which shall become liens upon said real estate or any part thereof. If White fails to pay any such taxes or such special assessments before any penalty or interest accrues thereon, or when the same may or should be paid, or if said real estate, or any part thereof, be sold for nonpayment of taxes or special assessments, then Black may, at its option, declare this contract null and void, or, in the alternative, pay such taxes and redeem said real estate. If Black pays such taxes or redeems said real estate, then the amounts paid by Black shall be added to the then unpaid principal balance of the purchase price and shall bear interest at the rate of five (5) percent per annum until paid.

5. *Partial Releases and Conveyances.* Said real estate is undeveloped and unimproved land. For the purpose of identifying the same and to facilitate the procedure by which the same may be conveyed in smaller tracts to the assignees of White, Black has drafted two (2) plats delineating thereon the various portions to be sold or dedicated to public use designated Tomahawk Estates and Tomahawk Hills respectively, copies of which said plats are attached hereto, marked Exhibits A and B respectively, and are made a part hereof. White shall complete the calculations and drafting of the Tomahawk Hills plat, and shall, at its own expense, cause said plat to be duly filed and recorded. White may assign and sell any whole lot shown on said plats but not less than a whole lot, and the purchase price therefore shall be not less than that indicated upon said exhibits as hereto attached, any such sale shall be for cash or under a contract by which the interest of White shall be assigned to the purchaser of such lot and Black shall convey by Special Warranty Deed, its interest in any such lot to the purchaser thereof, upon full payment of not less than the stipulated purchase price of said lot, which Special Warranty Deed shall be prepared by White and submitted to Black for execution. White shall pay all costs and expenses including recording fee and revenue stamps on each such conveyance. If said contract between White and any such buyer shall be for the purchase of said lot upon an installment basis, then the installment payments shall be not less frequent than equal monthly installments extending over a period of not more than four (4) years from the date of such contract of sale, and shall provide that if default in said payments shall be made for a period of ninety (90) days or more, said contract of sale to said purchaser shall be void.

6. *Monthly Reports.* During the period that this contract between Black and White shall be in effect, White shall, on or before the 15th day of each month, deliver to Black an executed, or facsimile copy of each said lot sale contract executed during the prior month. All

payments made by any such lot purchaser shall be divided into two equal sums, one of which shall be retained by White, the other of which shall be paid and delivered by White to Black with White's monthly report hereafter referred to, in payment of its then outstanding interest obligation, if any, upon the obligation hereby created, and the balance of which shall be applied in reduction of the then remaining principal balance of said obligation. White shall render to Black a regular monthly accounting statement of all of the said items by not later than the 15th day of the next following month. Said statement shall contain a complete listing of the names and addresses of all purchasers, the lot numbers of lots purchased, the contract price, the payments to date, an itemization of the amounts included in the payment accompanying the current statement, and the balance due on each contract, with a statement as to the total payment made to date by White to Black, including the application of those payments to interest and to principal, and the then current balance due. Said Black shall have the right from time to time and at all reasonable times, during ordinary business hours, to have its accountants, Smith and Smith, of Plain Village, Kansas, or any other agent designated by it, audit all books and records of White to ascertain the authenticity and correctness of the monthly reports from time to time rendered by White provided, however, that in all events such audit shall be at the expense of Black.

7. *Sale of Lots by Class Areas.* Notwithstanding any other provision hereof, the plat of Tomahawk Hills and Tomahawk Estates, as hereto attached, having been divided into three areas, designated respectively Class A, Class B and Class C areas, the sale of lots within said Tomahawk Hills and Tomahawk Estates shall be so limited that for each lot sold in the Class A area, White shall sell six (6) lots in the Class C area, and for each lot sold in the Class B area, White shall sell three (3) lots in the Class C area, and no sale of lots contrary to the provisions hereof in this respect shall be valid without the specific written approval of Black. Black shall not be obligated to release lots from the terms of this contract or to execute Special Warranty Deeds to the assignees of White for lots sold except upon the basis of one (1) Class A lot for every six (6) Class C lots and one (1) Class B lot for every three (3) Class C lots.

8. *Interim Payment on Sale of all but One Hundred Lots.* At such time as all but one hundred (100) lots in Tomahawk Hills and Tomahawk Estates are subject to executed contracts to purchase between White or its assignees, White shall pay to Black, in cash, the difference, if any, between the balance due on the unpaid purchase price as set forth in paragraph 1 hereof including interest and taxes and the value of the remaining lots in Tomahawk Hills and Tomahawk Estates based upon the aggregate of fifty (50) percent of their stipulated purchase price. In the alternative, the parties may agree to and apportion said difference among the remaining lots thereby

increasing the stipulated purchase price for each lot. In default of agreement Black may, at its option, declare the contract null and void and proceed under the terms and conditions of paragraph 10 hereof or may apportion said difference equally among the remaining one hundred (100) lots, thereby increasing the stipulated purchase price thereof sufficient to insure the payment of the balance due on the contract price as set forth in paragraph 1 hereof.

9. *Possession.* White shall have the possession of the above described property from and after the date hereof and for so long as this contract is in full force and effect.

10. *Default.* In the event White fails to comply with any of the terms of this agreement or in the event White fails either to sell two hundred (200) lots or to reduce the unpaid balance of the purchase price to One Hundred Thirty Thousand and 00/100 ($130,000) Dollars by July 1, 19___, or if White fails either to sell four hundred (400) lots or to reduce the unpaid balance of the purchase price to One Hundred Ten Thousand and 00/100 ($110,000) Dollars by July 1, 19___, or if White fails either to sell six hundred (600) lots or to reduce the unpaid balance of the purchase price to Ninety Thousand and 00/100 ($90,000) Dollars by July 1, 19___, or if White fails either to sell eight hundred (800) lots or to reduce the unpaid balance of the purchase price to Seventy Thousand and 00/100 ($70,000) Dollars by July 1, 19___, or if White fails either to sell one thousand (1,000) lots or to reduce the unpaid balance of the purchase price to Fifty Thousand and 00/00 ($50,000) Dollars by July 1, 19___, or if White fails to pay the purchase price in full on or before January 1, 19___, this contract shall, at the option of Black, be and become null and void. Under this contract a lot will be considered to have been sold for the purpose of determining the number of lots sold on the dates hereinbefore set forth in this paragraph 10, if any assignment contract has been executed for the purchase of said lot in accordance with the terms and conditions of this contract and each said assignment contract is in full force and effect on the date of determination of the number of lots sold, notwithstanding the fact that at a subsequent date the assignment contract may become null and void by virtue of nonpayment of the installments by the purchaser. On each date of determination of the number of lots sold as hereinbefore stated, only contracts on each such date in full force and effect, and not in default, will be considered as constituting a sale under the provisions of the paragraph.

If Black declares this contract null and void by written notice to White, all sales efforts by White shall cease and Black shall be entitled to immediate possession of all unsold lots.

Black shall give White thirty (30) days written notice of its election to declare this contract in default and to repossess all lots then unsold. Failure to give such notice shall constitute a waiver of such event of default, but shall not constitute a waiver of any subsequent event of default.

Upon repossession, this contract shall be terminated and be thereafter null and void, and White shall forthwith deliver to Black all plats, surveys, abstracts, maps and other materials and information which it now has and may hereafter acquire, regarding the above described property. Notwithstanding such default and/or repossession, all payments thereafter accruing under assignment contracts then in force shall continue to be divided, fifty (50) percent to be retained by White and fifty (50) percent to be paid by White to Black until final payment, or default in payment, is made by the last remaining assignee of White.

11. *Obligation of White.* White shall exert its best efforts in the advertising, promotion and sale lots in the real property hereinbefore described and shall construct such roads as may be necessary, in the exercise of the sole and uncontrolled discretion of White, on rights-of-way as dedicated in said plats, and shall keep said roads and the real property hereinbefore described free and clear of liens and encumbrances.

12. *Representations.* It is understood and agreed that this contract does not create or purport to create an agency relationship between Black and White; that White is not authorized to make any representation for and on behalf of Black; that Black is not bound by any representation made by White; that in the event it should be necessary or required that any sum be repaid to White's assignee, such sum shall be repaid by White and that Black has no obligation to repay to White's assignee any sum of money which it may receive under or by virtue of the terms and conditions of this contract; that Black in no event shall be obligated to deliver any deed of conveyance to White or White's assignee, except as herein set forth and except on full payment by White's assignee of not less than the stipulated purchase price for each lot and except on actual receipt by Black of not less than fifty (50) percent of the stipulated purchase price on each lot and White promises and agrees to save and hold Black harmless from any and all loss which Black may sustain by virtue of White's failure to abide by the terms and provisions of this paragraph in particular and this contract in general.

13. *Bankruptcy or Dissolution.* In the event of the insolvency, bankruptcy or corporate dissolution of White, this contract shall, at the option of Black, be and become null and void. Upon the happening of any of said events, a default shall occur and the termination of rights under this contract shall proceed as hereinbefore set forth in paragraph 9 hereof.

14. *Entitlement to Rent.* In the event that White should rent any portion or all of the above described property, fifty percent (50%) of the rental received by White or fifty percent (50%) of the value of the rental received by White, if the rental is paid in kind, shall be paid to Black in the same manner as hereinbefore provided for payment of installments on the purchase price of lots.

15. *Final Settlement.* When White shall have paid Black in full all

principal, interest and tax advancements due from White to Black hereunder, said Escrow Agent shall deliver said Warranty Deed to White, which shall forthwith cause the same to be filed for record and recorded in the office of the Recorder of Deeds of Stone County, Missouri, at White's expense, but White shall then and there be entitled to reimbursement from Black of the cost of any Revenue Stamps required by law to be fixed to said deed.

16. *Binding on Successors and Assigns.* This contract shall extend to and be binding upon the successors and assigns of the parties hereto.

IN WITNESS WHEREOF, the parties hereto have caused these presents to be executed by their respective Presidents and attested by their respective Secretaries and have caused their corporate seals to be affixed hereto, the day and year first above written.

BLACK DEVELOPMENT CO., INC.

BY_____

President

ATTEST

_____ WHITE, INC.

   Secretary   BY_____

                   President

ATTEST

_____

   Secretary

I have received income from this project for many years. The original owners have received substantial profitable income during the same years.

Here is an example of the land dealer obtaining control of land without any investment in the land. Then, through his knowledge of the system, the dealer is able to make a substantial profit for all concerned. Money talks; reputation and experience also speak for the land dealer. You can make your reputation take the place of investment cash in your land deals.

USE THE SELLER'S CREDIT

The seller generally wants to sell his property. This desire on his part can be used to help make it possible for you to buy. Many owners of land are also successful farmers, professional, or business men. Their financial position may make it easy for them to obtain a loan on the property you wish to buy.

Here you approach the seller in much the same manner you would any loan source. You present your plan for converting the land to new and profitable use. You show your personal and financial status. After establishing your position in the seller's mind, you explain that if he desires to obtain a substantial amount of cash at the time of the sale he could do the following.

YOU RECOMMEND THE PLAN

The sale price of the property is $20,000. You, the buyer, will pay $2,000 down payment. The seller obtains a loan from his loan source of $10,000; as this $10,000 is a loan, the seller will get this money tax free. This gives the seller $12,000 in cash. You, the buyer, sign a *Contract for Deed* with an arrangement at a bank so that you send the payments to the bank and the bank disburses the money as per a written agreement. This arrangement is made so you are certain that the seller's loan payments are made.

Your purchase contract is for $18,000, which is the balance of the land price after deducting your $2,000 down payment. You will, of course, pay interest. As you make your payments, the seller's loan is paid off and at the end of the contract time, you will have a clear title to the land. Be sure that the original loan obtained by the seller is drawn with release and prepayment clauses so it allows you to follow your planned use of the land.

YOU SHOW THE WAY

Here you have shown the seller how he can have a large cash income at the time of the sale. He can have income over a number of years, and he can make an extra profit from the interest you pay. This is another example of being able to buy the land you want by offering the solution to the seller's problem or meeting his cash requirements.

You have used the seller's credit to finance your land deal.

EXAMPLES OF PROFITS FROM BUYING RIGHT
CASH MAKES A PROFIT

Using cash obtained as shown in this chapter, you buy the land you want at 25 percent less than the price would have been if you obtain terms from the seller. All of that 25 percent is profit. On a $10,000 purchase you make a profit of $2,500 on the day you buy the land. Here the profit in your pocket is not from selling: this is a profit from buying right.

TERMS MAKE THE DEAL POSSIBLE

Buying on terms may be your only road to profit if you have only a small amount of cash, or if your cash will be needed to put your sales plan into action. Knowing how to obtain the best terms at the lowest cost will put you in the land business. You can't profit in land unless you deal in land. You buy land to make that profit. Terms can be the answer; terms can be the right way to buy land.

NO CASH DEALS

You have learned that no cash deals in land are possible. In fact, deals that require you to pay only a percentage of the sales income can be arranged. It is virtually impossible to do anything but profit from such no cash deals with the payments out of income.

Once you have experience and reputation, you can and will find these no cash deals. That is, you will find them if you know how they work, and how to explain them to a land owner.

Do not depend on the land owner knowing how to put together a deal. If he knew these things, he might not sell at all. He might do the things you plan to do, and make the profits you will make.

You are the expert in your own deal. No one will know it better; no one will have its interest at heart as much as you. Depend on your knowledge. Depend on yourself. Any help you get from others is to be appreciated, but not expected.

BUYING RIGHT GUARANTEES PROFIT

You, the dealer in land, must buy right to guarantee your profit. You can buy right if you know the way. You can easily find buy-right opportunities if you do the following.

1. Study the system
2. Know your product

3. Decide where to buy
4. Have a planned use
5. Check and test
6. Use the buying chart
7. Put the methods outlined in this book to work for you.
Do the above and your *fortune in land* is virtually assured.

5

Options and How to Use Them to Your Advantage

Now you will learn the least known method of dealing in land with little or no capital. In this chapter you will learn what an option is; more important, you will learn the many and varied uses of options. You will learn how you, the dealer in land, can actually eliminate financial risk through the use of options.

OPTIONS DEFINED

An option is a contract or agreement where the owner of property gives to a person or business entity, for a period of time, the right to purchase his property for a specified amount of money, on specified terms and with certain prescribed conditions.

There is a monetary consideration—it can be as little as one dollar, and even that does not actually have to be paid. The monetary consideration must be recited in the option agreement. The option agreement must be in writing to be binding. Time is the essence of an option agreement.

If an option is not exercised in the specified time, it automatically ceases to exist.

LEGAL POINTS

(Check with your lawyer; the laws change; the laws are different in various states.)

1. An option must be in writing.
2. It should recite the consideration.
3. It should clearly spell out the entire purchase agreement.
4. Time is of the essence; the expiration date must be clearly stated.
5. If the seller is married, the signature of the spouse should be on the option.
6. If the option is extended or renewed by written instrument, there must be evidence of additional consideration.
7. An option can be assigned.

REASONS FOR OPTIONS

The basic reason an option form is used is to give the buyer, in return for a consideration, the right to a specified period of time to determine if he wants to purchase the property.

During the time period of the option, the owner cannot sell the property to another buyer. In fact, the property described in the option is withdrawn from the market for the period covered by the option. If the option holder decides against completing the purchase, he forfeits the money paid for the option. If he decides to complete the purchase, the option money is applied as a credit to the purchase of the property.

ORDINARY OPTIONS IN USE

You have found the piece of land you feel is right for your plan. The price and terms are satisfactory. You have one problem—you want to be certain that your planned use is practical. You wish to investigate the market for your planned use of the land; you need time.

An option can give you that time safely, and generally at very little cost. Because you do not want to take the chance that the owners will sell to someone else while you do your checking, you ask for an option on the land.

The seller will probably be willing to give you an option. He will ask for a monetary consideration. Here you must negotiate; the name of this game is pay as little as possible for the option. Keep in mind that if you do not complete the purchase, you will forfeit the money you have put up for the option.

No two options are identical; no two sellers are the same. You must negotiate as best you can, to get the longest option for the least money. You should always try to get a no money option, if possible.

Here, you know that to use an ordinary option you simply negotiate the option that suits your need.

Next, why use an ordinary option. Again, the answer is simple. You need time; you buy that time with an option.

The ordinary standard option is an important tool in dealing in land. It can make it possible for you to check and test before making the actual purchase.

SPECIAL OPTIONS

The *Rolling Option:* here you buy the land on the basis of an initial purchase of part of the land with an option that can be exercised for additional portions of the land at stated time intervals. We will use an example of how such a deal might work.

> The seller has 100 acres of land. He wants $500 per acre—total price $50,000. You have planned use that will result in your subdividing each acre into three residential building sites. You have $10,000 in cash. You will need to have the land surveyed; you will need to put in streets; you will need money for advertising and sales promotion.

You can readily see that it would be virtually impossible for you to handle this deal through an outright purchase of the land.

That is the reason for the use of a *Rolling Option.* Using the rolling option, you pay the seller $5,000 and receive title to ten acres of the land. You also receive an option on the balance of the land. The option you obtain is not an ordinary option, it is a rolling option. This rolling option states as follows.

> One hundred and eighty days from the date of this option, providing the buyer has paid the sum of $5,000, the seller will deliver to the

buyer title to 10 acres of land, said land being described as tract "B" on the attached plat which plat is considered part of this option agreement.

It is further agreed that each one hundred and eighty days thereafter, providing that the buyer pays $5,000 on or before the end of each such period, the seller will deliver title to succeeding ten acre tracts shown as tracts C through J, such title to be on tracts in alphabetical order. This will continue until the total sum of $45,000 has been paid and title to all tracts has been delivered to the buyer.

In the event the buyer shall default on the payments as prescribed in this option, this option shall be null and void and the seller will have no further need to deed any property to the buyer, nor shall there be any liability between the buyer and the seller.

ADVANTAGES TO THE BUYER

The use of this special rolling type option gives you, the spare time land dealer, a number of advantages. It makes a $50,000 land purchase possible with only $5,000 in cash. It leaves you part of your capital to spend for improvements and sales expense.

It allows you to test the profitable salability of this specific land with a minimum dollar investment and a corresponding minimum risk. It allows you to stop at any time without your incurring additional liability to the seller. If you had purchased the land on a mortgage, you would not have this liability protection.

In addition, you could actually profit from the first ten acres and then for reasons of your own decide not to continue. You could do this and not owe the seller any money or have any liability.

Here you have taken all the land off the market. You can test the sales, test the profits, then decide to stop or proceed. The rolling option has made this reduced risk deal possible.

NO CASH OPTIONS

It is legal for the land owner to give you an option without your paying him any money. If the seller wishes to help make your purchase of his land possible, he may be willing to give you an option without any payment.

The main desire of most sellers is to make the sale. If giving you an option for 30 to 90 days or even longer will help make the sale, if the seller doesn't have another buyer in sight, he has very little to lose by granting you an option. An option does not allow you to do anything to or with the property. The only thing the seller is giving you is time. His only risk is that a buyer will come along during the option period and he will not be able to make the sale.

No cash options are much more common than most people dealing in real estate will admit. Real estate agents are not anxious for this knowledge to spread. It is to their interest to only deal in options that involve a monetary consideration.

You, the dealer in land, should know this—no money options are common—sometimes, all it takes to get one is to ask. You have nothing to lose when you ask the seller for a no money option; all he can say is no, and he may say yes.

THE NO OPTION, OPTION

You won't find the next method of dealing in real estate in any other book. At least I have never found any written reference to the method I have named the *No Option, Option.*

I have used this method a number of times, and to date all uses have resulted in profitable deals in land. I will describe the method by relating an actual deal from its beginning to its profitable conclusion.

I was looking for a resort land investment opportunity. Unfortunately, when I found it, the owner was talking all cash, and I was in a low cash position and my personal lines of credit were extended as far as I felt was prudent.

I HAD EVERYTHING BUT THE MONEY

I had the time; I had the property located; I had the plan; I was short the money. I put the no option, option method into operation. I approached the land owner on this basis. Would he agree verbally to sell me the property at so much an acre, if I paid all cash. As the offering price was the price I knew he wanted, he readily agreed. I then asked him if he would verbally agree to allow me ninety days in which to raise the cash. Would he promise not to sell in that period to anyone else? With some reluctance he agreed.

THE VERBAL OPTION

I now had a verbal option to buy the land at a stipulated price per acre. On the basis of this verbal option, I had ninety days in which to raise the money. This verbal option would be impossible to enforce in law. In fact, if the seller decided to sell during the ninety day period, there would be nothing I could do about it.

MOST PEOPLE KEEP THEIR WORD

In the eyes of the law, I did not have a legal enforceable option. All I had was the owner's word. This is the reason I call this method the no option, option. You have no option, yet if the owner's word is good you have all of the benefits of an option.

It is my personal experience that most people keep their word. This is a point of pride with many persons. The old saying, "my word is my bond," is applicable today, if care is exercised on how it is applied.

In this case of the no option, option method, you are investing only your time. If the owner was to go back on his word, you would not lose any money. You would lose your time, and if he went back on his word at the last minute, you might lose a little face.

HOW TO PROFIT FROM A VERBAL OPTION

Now to the why we wanted the verbal option. I had a group of men who had contacted me relative to investing in a land deal. I now approached them with my no option, option deal.

I had maps of the land, I had sales and profit projections, and I had my verbal option. Based on my presentation, these men and I visited the land. The owner, feeling that he had a buyer in me, was most cordial and helpful. This helped convince the investors that I had control of the land. It also stopped one of the investors from trying to purchase the land on his own.

I entered into an agreement with these investors. They put up both the purchase money and the money for subdividing. The owner honored his verbal option, and the land was purchased. The planned use was put into effect.

PROFIT FOR ALL

The original owner was happy; he received his price per acre. The investors were happy; they received a substantial return on their investment. I was happy, as I had been able to deal profitably in land with only my time and knowledge of the method as my investment.

Here, using the no option, option method of dealing in land, everyone made a profit. Here the dealer in land created action, created value, created profit.

PROFIT FROM LAND YOU NEVER BUY

It is possible to profit from dealing in land, yet never own any land. You are not required to have a real estate sales or broker's license, as you do not sell the land.

SELL THE OPTION

You in effect sell the option; in legal terms, you assign the option. During the time period of an option, the person holding the option controls the land as far as its sale is concerned. The owner of the land has in effect sold the sale rights to the property for the time period of the option.

WHO BUYS THE OPTION

In my example, using the no option, option method, I mentioned that one of the investors was interested in buying the land on his own. This man was in the process of changing from an investor into a dealer.

This man now became a prospect to buy a land option. Because he was in the initial learning stage of dealing in land, he wanted to be shown how to convert land into profit. He wanted someone to show him how to do it. He wanted and needed a use of the land plan.

SELL THE PLAN, NOT THE LAND

You find the land; you develop the plan; you option the land; this time get your option in writing; get it for the longest possible length of time.

Now you approach this man, and present the land the plan. Show him exactly how he should proceed. Take him step by step to the profit in your plan for the land. Sell him on the plan, then explain that you are willing to assign the option to him. Ask for so much money or participation in the profits for this assignment of the option.

WHY SELL THE OPTION

This man may well ask, if this is such a good plan, if the profits are so assured, why are you willing to sell your option.

The answer is money, or more truthfully, the lack of it. You exert your time and your knowledge in a deal such as this to help improve your cash position. If you are in a good cash position, or if your lines of credit are open, you would in all probability exercise the option yourself. You would put your plan into action, and make all the profits for yourself.

Unfortunately, you may not always be in a good financial position. Here, using an option, you can practice your chosen vocation, and do so at a profit. You can deal in land you never own; you can do this with practically no investment, and you can make a profit.

YOU CAN PROFIT FROM OPTIONS IF

You can do any and all of the things outlined in this chapter; you can in fact do much more, *if*. The if is, if you—
1. Understand what an option is.

2. Understand how options work.

3. Understand that there are many kinds of options.

4. Understand how to obtain options.

5. Understand that an option is not always what it seems.

The way to understanding is study and practice. The land dealer should study, plan, test, and then deal. This chapter has given you a start in the use of options. Further study and practice can make you the expert in options.

BAD DEAL AVOIDED BY USE OF AN OPTION

The author, after much searching, found a piece of land that seemed ideal for his land sale plan. The owner was represented by a Realtor. The total price and terms were agreed upon. An option was drawn based on the agreed price and terms, plus the ability of the owner to deliver a clear title to all the acreage agreed upon.

Subsequent investigation determined that the landowner seemed to have either deliberately or accidentally exaggerated the number of acres in the tract. There also was a boundary dispute possibility between one of the adjoining landowners.

The purchase was not consummated. No money changed hands and the author was saved from a bad deal because he had used an option to purchase. It should be understood that the reason for the option was to gain time to check the feasibility of the land sales plan. The checking of the title and acreage would have been done in a non-option purchase of the land. Here the option actually served two purposes.

A $1,000 OPTION GETS 10 PERCENT OF A MILLION DOLLARS

Mr. S. paid $1,000 for an option on a prime piece of urban property. Total price of the land was $50,000. Mr. S., after getting the option, developed a plan to use the land as the site of a medical building. Mr. S. sold the land option and the plan to a group of doctors for $50,000 cash and ten percent of the owner corporation. The corporation built a one million dollar medical center building on the land. Mr. S. now has 10 percent of a million dollar property without one dollar invested. The cash he received even returned his option money. Here an option and a plan makes a big deal possible with only $1,000 in cash, and even that is returned.

6

Zoning: Your Key
to Big Profits

Zoning can be the key factor that overnight can change the value of a piece of land. The actions of a zoning board in one meeting can and often do make fortunes for land owners.

To make zoning work to create profits you must understand the basics of what zoning is, how it works, and the how and why of zoning changes. This chapter will define, explain, and by example show, the many facets of how zoning can help make your fortune in land.

ZONING DEFINED

Zoning Ordinances regulate the character and use of property. They are imposed under the police power of the state.

Variances or Rezoning can be granted where the existing zoning law creates an undue hardship on the owner.

Zoning itself is the partition by ordinance of an area into zones reserved for different *purposes,* such as business, residential, multi-family, etc. Zoning is generally part of a master plan.

An example of zoning would be the neighborhood in which you now live. It is probably zoned for a single family dwelling per lot. This means neither you nor your neighbor can build an apartment building, factory, office building, or anything except a single family residence, and even that will be subject to certain restrictions as to type, size, distance from front, side and back property lines, etc.

This zoning keeps you from waking up one morning to find your neighbor has started a factory next to your home. Your neighbor has this same protection.

If you live in an apartment or town house complex, the zoning would be as follows: a master plan of multiple occupancy building approved by the appropriate zoning and planning board or boards.

In this master plan you might find a statement of the number of units, height of buildings, size of units, parking space per unit, etc. There would, in addition to the zoning, probably be a recorded set of restrictions. Restrictions can and in many cases do control land use in more detail than does zoning.

Zoning is both necessary and desirable. It serves the public welfare and is the legitimate use of the police powers vested in our governments. Improper zoning and zoning done maliciously or for personal, political, or financial gain by those controlling the zoning is not only immoral, it is in most cases illegal.

Zoning is neither infallible nor unchangeable. Zoning can be changed for any number of reasons. In this area of rezoning, the land dealer will find his opportunity for profit. Change the use and create value. Rezoning can change the use.

ZONING RECAP

1. Zoning is the partitioning by ordinance of an area into zones where the use of the land or property is controlled.
2. Zoning is the right under the law to control the type of use that may be made of a certain property.
3. Proper zoning is both necessary and beneficial to the general public.
4. Zoning can be changed.

WHO CONTROLS ZONING

State laws authorize zoning by communities as part of their master development plan. Zoning is accomplished by ordinance and most zoning is done by a zoning board, commission, or designated group, whose members are charged with the duty of interpreting and enforcing the zoning ordinances. This zoning board or commission may have subcommittees specifically designated to study and recommend changes, variances, and exceptions to the existing zoning regulations.

TIMES CHANGE

As an area develops over a period of many years, certain changes occur. These changes may make the original development plan obsolete. If the development plan is obsolete, then in all probability the zoning based on that original plan is obsolete.

These changes can be the opportunity the dealer in land is looking for. The changes can be the valid reason for a change in the zoning of a specific piece of land. Watch for signs of changing uses in an area. Visualize what is needed on today's market that was not needed when that area was zoned.

In the changing needs you may find the reason for asking for and receiving a variance, or change in zoning.

ZONING CAN BE CHANGED

A zoning change request or a request for a zoning variance must be made at a meeting of the zoning board or that body designated to hear zoning appeals. Such a request should be based on a good reason for the change in zoning. The request should be backed with facts to substantiate and validate the change request. An example of such a request happened to a friend of mind, Mr. E.T.

Mr. E.T. owned a large corner lot in a small but highly restricted suburban community. This lot was zoned for one single family dwelling. At the time Mr. E.T. purchased this lot, the surrounding area was all vacant land. The lots on the other three corners were, however, not in the same community as Mr. E.T.'s lot.

As time went by the entire area developed, and Mr. E.T. held his lot for value appreciation. The land across the street from Mr. E.T.'s lot was developed into a shopping center. This could be done because there had been no restrictive zoning on any of the land on the three corners facing Mr. E.T.'s lot.

After approximately ten years of owning his lot, Mr. E.T. found he was faced with this situation. He owned a large lot on a four-way intersection of what had become a heavy traffic street. The lots on the other three corners had been zoned commercial and sold for business purposes. One lot now had a drive-in restaurant; the other two corner lots had operating filling stations.

Mr. E.T's lot, because it was under a different community zoning ordinance, was still zoned single family residence. Mr. E.T. could not find a buyer for his lot. No one wanted to have their residence facing such a group of business establishments as now existed across from Mr. E.T.'s lot.

Mr. E.T. was being approached by oil companies, franchise food operators, and others to sell or lease his lot for commercial use. When these prospective buyers learned of the zoning, they, of course, revised their offers to contingency offers.

A contingency offer is where a sale or lease is made contingent upon a certain action taking place prior to the actual closing of the sale or the execution of the lease. In this case the contingency was, of course, the change of the zoning from residential to commercial.

Mr. E.T. applied to the zoning board for a change in zoning based on hardship. Hardship is defined as a condition where the existing zoning is working a hardship on the property owner. Hardship must be proven, and even when hardship is proven, if the zoning change would be detrimental to the public, then the zoning change in most cases would be denied. We must accept the fact that we are dealing with a concept of public good over the rights of an individual.

Mr. E.T's application for a change in zoning was denied. Mr. E.T. now had a lot that literally could not be sold at any price. Mr. E.T. filed an appeal; again, he was turned down. It was a number of years later that a change in administration in the community resulted in a new zoning board being appointed. Mr. E.T. applied to this new board; he presented his hardship case and his lot was rezoned commercial.

Mr. E.T. then sold his lot for hundreds of times the amount he had originally paid for it. Even with interest, taxes, and other expenses over the years of ownership, Mr. E.T. was able to realize a substantial profit. That profit resulted from the rezoning—nothing else could have created this value. Without the commercial zoning, Mr. E.T.'s lot would still be virtually worthless. Yes, zoning is the key to profit in many land deals.

HOW TO APPLY FOR A ZONING CHANGE

To understand how to apply for a zoning change or variance, you need to have a picture in your mind regarding the actual operations of a zoning board. To help you obtain this mental picture, the following is an item taken from a newspaper. Only the names and addresses have been omitted.

COUNCIL REFUSES OFFICE ZONING

The blank City Council has refused to rezone a tract near blank Street and blank Street for two office buildings and a branch post office structure. Several nearby residents objected to the rezoning. The proposal had been recommended for denial by the City Planning Commission.

The Council also denied duplex zoning for the southeast corner of blank Street. It granted planned apartment zoning for the blank apartments at blank and blank Streets. Approved rezoning at blank and blank Streets to permit parking for an already approved planned office building.

Here we see denials and approvals of zoning and rezoning, all in one session of a City Council meeting. Note the reference to the City Planning Commission. Such a planning commission is used to do studies of requests for rezoning, and based on these studies to recommend denial or approval. The zoning board or council is not required to follow these recommendations; however, they generally do follow them.

ATTEND ZONING HEARINGS

One of the best ways to understand how zoning changes can be obtained is to sit in on actual zoning board or City Council meetings when zoning requests are being considered. At such meetings you will be able to get the feel of the members and their attitudes toward various reasons for rezoning.

Knowledge is always an asset. The more knowledge you have regarding the operation of the zoning and planning group in your area, the better the chance you have to obtain affirmative action on your request for a rezoning or a variance.

MAKING YOUR APPLICATION

Prepare your facts in a clear, concise, and logical manner. Be ready to prove each fact. Have exhibits, maps, traffic counts, references, and anything that you feel will bolster your position.

Have an experienced attorney guiding you. Be courteous, and above all do not lose your temper. You may not receive courtesy. You may even be subjected to the bad manners and bad temper of a member or even members of the zoning group. I repeat, do not lose your temper; keep yourself under control.

You are appearing before these persons to accomplish a purpose that may literally make your fortune. You need the good will of all present. Be polite, state your facts, be ready to answer questions, and you just may get the zoning, rezoning, or variance that will make you a profitable land deal.

REVIEW OF PROCEDURE

1. Present the reason for the requested change in zoning.
2. Show that the change in zoning would not be harmful to others.
3. Present and prove your position with substantiating evidence.
4. Be prepared to answer all questions factually.
5. Be courteous; do not lose your temper.
6. Use an experienced, competent attorney, preferably one familiar with the zoning board members.

USE OF LAW, LOGIC, AND PERSUASION

We live in an imperfect world. Right and logic do not always prevail. One man or woman on a zoning board can, because of personal predjudice, ignore the law and the logic of a rezoning request and vote it down, or for the same wrong reason approve it.

We are dealing with a majority rules situation on most zoning boards. It cannot, however, be ignored that there are individual members of many zoning boards whose powers are greater than those of other members. These members can and do sway the actions of the entire board, and in the worst of cases actually control the board and its actions.

We have talked of presenting the facts to obtain rezoning. We have talked of being logical. We must now consider being persuasive. If you do not consider yourself persuasive, or if, because of the composition of the zoning board, you feel you would not be able to present your request in the most persuasive manner, then have someone else appear for you.

KEEP YOUR COOL

We discussed that you must not lose your temper. You must not even show irritation. You must remain in complete cotrol of your emotions. If you are by nature a person who loses control of himself under stress, then for your own good have someone other than yourself represent you before the zoning board.

A person is always more emotionally involved in his own deal. Your lawyer, for example, will not have this emotional involvement problem. In general another person, especially an experienced lawyer, can represent you and your case better than you can.

In many cases both you and your lawyer will present your request for rezoning. Both of you will be available to answer the board's questions. Let your lawyer retain control of your presentation. It is of extreme importance that it does not appear that you and the zoning board are on opposing sides. Such an appearance of two opposing sides may make the board feel that a decision in your favor is a loss to the board. You should strive to achieve a feeling that a decision in your favor is to the benefit of all concerned, or at the very least is not detrimental to anyone.

PROVE AND PERSUADE

The idea is for you to prove and persuade. It is your future and your profits that are at stake. An affirmative decision is the only objective. You are not trying to prove your personal superiority. You must persuade the zoning group that the change you are asking for is valid and legitimate.

The benefits you will receive from having your request approved is most certainly worth a well planned and properly executed presentation. If you plan carefully and if you know you made the best possible presentation, then, even if you receive a negative answer, you can be satisfied that you made your best effort.

NO CAN CHANGE TO YES

A resounding, even unanimous No vote on your request to have your land rezoned is not the end of it. There are, first of all, appeal procedures. There is also an opportunity to restudy and re-evaluate your side. Using the reasons given by the board for their negative answer, you can determine better arguments to be used in the future.

Time, changes in circumstances, new and different board members, area changes, etc., all can make the No of yesterday into the Yes of tomorrow. Remember Mr. E.T.—he was turned down twice; with him, the third time was the charm and the profit.

APPEALS FOR JUSTICE

You may appeal a zoning board's decision by taking your appeal to court. The court in general can only rule on whether the zoning board's decision was unreasonable or illegal. You will still be dealing with the question of the public interest.

Courts have declared some zoning ordinances invalid for a variety of reasons. All possible avenues that might lead to your obtaining that desired rezoning or variance should be explored. Persistence can be very profitable when it leads to that important affirmative action that converts your land investment into a land profit.

ZONING AS A LAND INVESTMENT TOOL

The following is a graphic illustration of creating value and profits by zoning. A land plan is developed for a real estate subdivision. Eighty percent of the land in this subdivision is platted into lots zoned single family residential. The developer ·sells these lots at cost, or even below cost. You are now asking the question, why would the developer be willing to break even or even lose money on these lots. The answer to your question is another example of zoning creating profits.

ZONED COMMERCIAL MAKES PROFITS

A piece of land zoned commercial in an area of no people will in general have a very low value. A restaurant, grocery store, filling station, etc., in a low population density area will in general hurt for lack of business.

The same piece of land, zoned commercial, and surrounded by hundreds or thousands of homes, each home having that great American user-consumer family inside, is a vastly different circumstance.

The developer, by making the residential property available at lowest possible cost to the buyer, has created the customers for the users of the 20 percent of his land he zoned commercial. Now, through the sale or lease of these commercial properties, the dealer in land profits, and these profits are directly related to these properties being zoned commercial. The zoning made the profits.

BUY WHERE ZONING SHOULD CHANGE

To find land where you may be able to obtain rezoning or zoning variances that will increase value, follow this plan of action:
1. Pick an area in which you wish to deal in land.
2. Study the original land use plan. This will be available from public records.
3. Get a breakdown of zoning for the specific area that interests you.
4. Study actions of the zoning board that governs this area. Study zoning changes, revisions, exceptions, and variances that have taken place since the original zoning ordinances were put into effect.

5. Look for changes in living and business patterns that could be reasons for a future zoning change.
6. See if you can find any land that in your opinion is zoned wrong.
7. Become acquainted with the personalities and backgrounds of the men who comprise the zoning board or committee.
8. Check if certain lawyers or law firms have a record of success in getting zoning changed in the area of your interest.

From this information you will be able to determine what, if any, profit from rezoning is available in your chosen area. Here study, research, knowledge, and planning are the keys to profits from zoning.

KNOW ZONING BEFORE YOU BUY

Before you buy any vacant land be certain that you know if it is zoned, and if so for what use it is zoned. Remember the following very important points.
1. Zoning restricts use.
2. Use creates value.
3. Zoning therefore controls value.
4. Rezoning or zoning variances change use, and therefore change value.

Zoning often is the major determining factor relating to the present and future value of land. Therefore, zoning is of major importance to anyone who deals or plans to deal in land.

A FINAL LOOK AT ZONING

Zoning is imposed under the police powers of the state. Zoning is for the public good. Zoning can be changed for valid reasons.

MR. B ZONES HIMSELF A FORTUNE

Mr. B was looking at retail lots being offered in a large subdivision on a lake. The seller of these lots was asking $3,000 to $5,000 for single family residential lots. Mr. B checked on the ownership of adjacent acreage. He found one 20 acre tract with a small amount of lake frontage was for sale. Mr. B was able to buy these 20 acres for $1,000 per acre, a total of $20,000, with a down payment of only $4,000 and release clauses in the purchase contract. Because the land was not in a controlled area, Mr. B was able to divide the land into tracts, and to zone these tracts for multi-family and business use. With the large residential subdivision next door, it was easy for Mr B to sell his commercially zoned tracts at very high prices. Last report had Mr. B with a substantial profit, and over half of his land still to sell. Here you make your own zoning, and with it your fortune.

7

Trades and Co-Ownership: Partners in Profit

The word *"trade"* in describing business, being in business, or the act of doing business, is derived from the following. Originally, business was conducted almost entirely through a system of barter and exchange. The trading of the product or service of one person for the product or service of another person was the first business method used by man. Trading pre-dates money, as we know it, by many centuries.

It is in the nature of man to trade or to exchange what he has for something he wants or needs. "Every man a horse trader" is in the oldest of American traditions. It is then little wonder that even in the world of today we find that trading can be of great advantage to the dealer in land.

WHY, WHAT, AND CONSEQUENCES

For the land dealer to take full advantage of the benefits of trading, he must know the *why, what,* and the consequences. The following three points are vital to a successful trade:

1. Know why you are trading instead of selling.
2. Know what you are getting and what you plan to do with the product or service you get.

3. Know the tax advantages or liabilities that will accrue as the result of the trade.

Trading, like buying and selling, is only good when done with knowledge and according to a plan. Know why you trade; know what you get, and know how you will profit. Then, and only then, make that trade.

HOW TO FIND TRADING OPPORTUNITIES

As in most real estate deals, a good source of potential trades will be through real estate brokers. In general, the dealer in land will have to be the guiding hand that moves and directs the broker in his efforts to find that just right trade deal. Keep in mind that it's your needs and your circumstances that are important. No one knows your situation as well as you do. You must be the one to put the broker in motion.

BEST SOURCE

The next source of trading opportunities is probably the best. It is the backbone of real estate buying, selling, and trading. It is the community newspaper. The advertising sections, both display and classified, of such papers carry more real estate advertising than all other sources combined. Here is one easy to obtain source of opportunities with enough details to allow a selection of those offerings that seem to fit the dealer's situation.

An example is the following list of trades offered in a Sunday issue of the Kansas City Star newspaper in its classified advertising section under the heading, "To Exchange Real Estate." Details are omitted:

1. Trade acreage for home
2. For Sale or Trade—Converted Home
3. Four Bedroom House for Farm
4. $10,000 equity in home for down payment on motel
5. Trade 80 acres improved farm for 40 acres unimproved and cash
6. Store Building, Trade, Your offer
7. Trade 20 improved acres for Home

8. Clear 40 acres for larger acreage
9. Trade Baby Grand Piano and Cash for Home
10. Building lots, want Mobile Home
11. Equity in apartments for acreage zoned apartments
12. Trade acreage for near new Tractor
13. Lake Lot, trade for Mowing Tractor
14. Near New Car for vacant ground, city or country

As you can see, there are many possibilities in this one Sunday edition. You, of course, can start your kind of trade action by running your own ad in the paper. Such an ad will in many cases result in replies from persons as interested in trading as you are. These ads can be very low in cost and can be amazingly productive.

WORD OF MOUTH

Contact with a real estate broker, using newspaper ads, and now by simply telling people what you have and what you want. Using conversations, phone calls, and letters to spread the word of your situation can and does get results.

TRADING LAND FOR LAND

When you, the land dealer, find you have land that has appreciated in value, you probably, if you sell at the new market value, will have an income tax problem. One solution to such a problem is a trade—that is, a like for like trade, or a land for land trade. These like for like trades can be accomplished with and without cash considerations.

Here is an example of such a trade. Mr. A bought 140 acres of land a number of years ago for $20,000. Today that land is valued at $40,000. Mr. A is in a fairly high income tax bracket from his regular income source. If Mr. A sells his land for cash he will incurr a very substantial tax liability, and a large portion of his profit will have to be paid in federal and state income taxes.

An installment sale would defer and probably reduce the tax burden. It would not, however, be as advantageous to Mr. A and his long-range plans as would the right trade.

Mr. A presents the following to a real estate broker. Mr. A is willing to trade his land for either larger acreage or land of a higher value. Mr. A tells the broker he will pay a cash difference if the right trade is available.

The following is the deal that was consummated.

Mr. A traded his 140 acres valued at $40,000 to Mr. B for Mr. B's 260 acres valued at $60,000. Mr. A paid Mr. B $20,000 in cash (it could have been part cash and a note, or all note).

Mr. A now has land valued at $60,000 at a cost to him of only $40,000 (his original $20,000 for his land and the $20,000 he paid to complete the deal). Mr. A has increased his net worth by $20,000, and he has incurred no tax liability until and unless he sells his new land at a price higher than his cost basis.

Here is a trade to increase worth by realizing the appreciated value of land you own, and at the same time not creating tax liability. This is an example of the reason a land for land trade can be part of the land dealer's plan for increasing assets and paying less taxes.

NO CASH NEEDED

Most dealers in land find themselves short of cash from time to time. The nature of dealing in land requires that the dealer have his capital in land he is holding for sale at a profit or for appreciation in value.

The dealer who wants to continue dealing to improve his asset value and even his profit position, and who is in a short cash position, will find that trading land for land offers many no cash deals. It will generally boil down to your ability to trade the land you have for land that you believe you can either now or in the future realize more profit from than the profits you can project from your present land.

It is possible to trade your land for another more valuable piece of land without paying any extra money. The reason this is possible is the desire and ability of one person to more profitably develop or sell a certain type of land.

An example of this is the following transaction. A person owned a number of vacant lots in a lakefront subdivision. This lakefront property was over 150 miles from the owner's home.

The owner was a spare time dealer in land and his full time occupation precluded his going to this land, except on infrequent occasions. This owner had a cost base in these lots of approximately $400 per lot.

The owner had been working with a real estate broker who lived in the subdivision. This broker had been handling all the sales of these lots. The broker passed away, and this left the owner without a sales force. His operation was too small to attract another qualified broker as a replacement.

A period of almost a year went by without a salesman and with, of course, very few sales. Even the sales that were made were made at very low prices. The owner was most anxious to make some change that would create a profit from these lots.

This owner was reading the classified advertising in the local paper. This was the ad that made a no cash deal that resulted in profits for both land owners.

> Trade, 50 acre Citrus Grove, located in Texas. Want lots on the Lake of the Ozarks. Name and Phone number.

The owner's lots were on Lake of the Ozarks, so he called the man. He learned that this man was selling lots in a number of small subdivisions on the Lake of the Ozarks. The man had acquired the citrus grove in trade and was not in a position to operate it. He readily agreed to trade the grove based on a price of $40,000, taking 50 of the lake lots as representing the $40,000. It was a straight trade of 50 lake lots for the 50 acre citrus grove.

The owner of the lake lots contacted a real estate broker in a city in Texas near the grove. The broker, after checking the situation, said he could sell the grove for $30,000.

The trade was consummated; the grove was sold for $30,000 which resulted in a $10,000 profit less the broker's commission. The new owner of the lake lots was able to add these lots to his inventory and, because he was already selling in the area, could and subsequently did sell these lots on a basis that returned him a substantial profit.

Both parties profited from this no cash trade of land for land because there was a special circumstance. The special circumstance was the ability of the owner of the grove to sell the lake lots easier and more profitably than could the original owner of the lake lots.

This is an example of how a no cash trade deal made thousands of dollars of profit for both parties in the trade.

TRADES FOR GOODS AND SERVICES

When you, the dealer in land have a specific need for a product or service, think "trade." It may be possible for you to trade a lot, an acre, or a tract of land for that product or service you need, and thereby reduce your cash outgo. Such a trade can also be a profit if your trading price is more than your cost base. Even with a break-even trade you are conserving your operating capital.

To initiate such trades you can, of course, advertise in the newspaper as outlined previously in this chapter. In this area of trading for goods or services it is in many cases better if you take a more direct approach.

By letter or phone, contact the person or company that can supply your need. Ask them if they would be interested in a trade. It is quite common practice for the land owner to trade land to the surveyor as payment in part or in full for the surveying work. Road builders and other suppliers of services and materials used in improving or subdividing land are prime trading possibilities.

REDUCES NEED FOR CASH

The trading of land can and often does include trades for cars, boats, airplanes, houses, and, in fact, almost anything that is also bought and sold. Keep in mind the possibilities of a trade whenever you are making a purchase. You will be surprised at the potential for getting the things you want without cash when you think "trade."

Special Note: Tax consequences from such trades are so varied that the only way you can be certain you pay the proper taxes will be for you to obtain advice from a tax consultant or the Internal Revenue Service on each specific trade.

TRADING HELPS SALES

A secondary benefit from trading for goods and services is the word of mouth advertising you receive. The person or company that now owns land in your project will tell others about it. Here you will have a free sales agent telling and selling people on your property.

The reason for this sales help is simply that this person knows that as your land values increase, so will his. This fact can also lead to other trade deals and, of course, to land sales.

CO-OWNERSHIP

Trading your property or services to another person or company in such a manner as to become a co-owner in a land project can be very profitable for the land dealer. A pooling of knowledge, resources, and desire can put a land deal across faster and better in many cases than the parties involved could do as individuals.

With one party furnishing the land, a second furnishing the knowledge, and with maybe one or a dozen persons putting up the operating capital, a large land development can be undertaken with minimum risk to all parties.

Co-ownership can be accomplished using a simple partnership, a limited partnership in syndicate form, or a corporation. The legal, liability, and tax considerations are of great importance in co-ownership of land. Here is the need for good legal advice, and always have all possible details in writing.

REGULAR CO-OWNERSHIP

You, the dealer in land, locate a tract of land and develop a plan to convert it into a profit. You do not have enough capital to buy this land and develop it. Here is where a partner, a group of partners, or a corporation can put you in business.

After selecting the land, compile all the costs, sales projections, and expected profits into an easy to understand portfolio. Now present this information to persons you feel would be interested in being involved in such a project.

You, as the promoter, are entitled to a percentage of the project for being the promoter. You may also want to put up part of the money so as to have a larger and possibly controlling interest in the project.

In such a co-ownership project, be as honest and above board as possible. Your reputation and possibly your future ability to deal in land is at stake. Honesty is not only the right thing as a moral value, it is also good business. Be sure you have the time and are willing to work to make this co-op venture a success. The other persons will be relying on you a great deal. They, in many cases, are putting a part of their life's savings into your project. This is a grave responsibility. If you are not sure that you can make the deal go, it might be better to settle for a lesser deal that you can handle alone.

Co-ownership deals are for the experienced land dealer if he is the promoter. It may be you will want to put your money into someone else's land deal. Remember, if you do that, he is the dealer and you are the investor. You can, however, use such a deal as your school to learn how to have your own land deal in the future.

PERFECT FOR SPARE TIME DEALER

Co-ownership can be the best type of land deal for the spare time dealer for a number of reasons. One, it reduces the capital required; two, it puts you in touch with the ideas and assistance of other persons; three, it uses the ability you have in your regular occupation to meet people who can join you in such a venture.

Before you finally decide on a co-ownership land deal, ask two questions:

1. Can I handle the deal alone?
2. Do I want to, in a sense, live with the other co-owners?

Co-ownership can be the fastest way for the dealer in land to really deal big, and big deals can be the road to big profits.

ONCE MORE FROM THE TOP

Trades can be profitable, save taxes, and not require cash. Co-ownership can make you a big dealer overnight. It's up to you to study, plan, and then make that trade or set up that partnership.

SPECIAL NOTE ON BROKERS

In certain cases of trading properties, the real estate broker will be entitled to receive a commission from both parties. If, however, one of the parties has an agreement with the broker to represent his interests in negotiating a trade for his property, the broker normally would not be able to represent the other party in the trade and would, therefore, not expect or be entitled to a commission from other than the party he has agreed to represent.

Be sure you have a clear understanding on this matter of who is represented by whom, who is to pay a commission, and who is entitled to that commission. A clear understanding at the outset can stop problems before they start.

SPECIAL TAX NOTICE

The subject matter of this chapter on "Trades and Co-ownership" has so many ramifications as to income taxes that no concise or simple answers can be given in this book. Consult a tax expert, the Internal Revenue Service, or your attorney *before* you make the deal.

YOUNG LAWYER MAKES $80,000 IN LAND

A young lawyer trades his legal work for a run down 80 acre farm. Using methods outlined in this book, he subdivides the land into lots. He sells these lots at retail and makes a profit in excess of $80,000. This profit was the result of only a few weeks' work and a small investment for initial surveying and advertising.

OLD LAWYER RETIRES

An old lawyer retires on one land deal. In this case the lawyer traded legal work on an estate settlement for land located at the intersection of two highways. This land was later sold for use as a shopping center. The sale price was so large and the profit so tax sheltered that the lawyer was able to retire from the proceeds. Here again a few weeks' work leads to financial independence. What else but land could perform such financial miracles?

CO-OWNERSHIP AND A TRADE MAKES EVERYBODY HAPPY

Co-ownership and a trade, both in one land deal with profits for all concerned. Mr. L wanted to get into land development on a lake. Mr. K, an experienced dealer in land, supplied the know-how while Mr. L did the work; they split the initial costs. The project was near the home of Mr. L; it was hundreds of miles from Mr. K. Using the knowledge and experience of Mr. K and the effort of Mr. L, the first year of this project was very successful. Mr. L decided he wanted the entire project for himself. Mr. L had all his cash tied up in his half of the original costs. Mr. L had a cabin cruiser. Mr. K wanted a cabin cruiser, so a trade of Mr. L's cabin cruiser for Mr. K's equity in the land deal was made. Two satisfied persons from using first co-ownership, then a trade.

Life can be exciting, enjoyable, and profitable when you know how to join with others in deals that serve all persons involved.

8

Secrets of Legal
Tax Avoidance

Lawyers charge from twenty to one hundred dollars and more per hour. It is easy to see that these charges can add up to big money fast. If you do not want to pay thousands of dollars to train a lawyer in real estate and tax laws, do the following.

HAVE TWO LAWYERS

Select one lawyer who has extensive experience in the legal aspects of real estate. Select your second lawyer based on his experience and knowledge of tax matters.

Now you have experts in the two most important areas for the dealer in land. It is virtually impossible for one lawyer to be an expert in both real estate and tax law. You may, however, find a law firm that has specialists in both fields.

LOCATING YOUR LAWYERS

Most clients are introduced to their lawyer by mutual friend or business associate. This is fine if your are looking for an attorney to handle general legal matters. The land dealer is not looking for a lawyer for all types of legal matters.

You, the dealer in land, must have a legal expert in real estate, and a legal expert in tax matters. Try very hard not to settle for less than an expert in each field.

THE BEST MAY COST LESS

The most experienced lawyer may be the most expensive by the hour, but he may be the least costly based on results obtained. There are no bargains in legal advice. The way to save legal costs will be explained in detail later in this chapter. The explanation will show you how to assist your lawyer handle your problems in the least amount of time. Lawyers generally charge on an hourly basis—save their time, save your money.

FINDING THE BEST LAWYER FOR YOU

Your friends, relatives, business associates, club members, etc., all may know the lawyer you need. Newspaper and magazines carry stories of lawyers handling real estate and tax matters. Using all of these sources, you will in time locate the lawyers that meet your needs.

COMPATIBILITY

Now establish if you and this human being are compatible. Keep in mind that a lawyer is a human being first and a lawyer second. If you do not like the human being, you probably will not be happy with the lawyer. You need rapport with your legal counsel; select lawyers you respect and like.

YOUR RELATIONSHIP WITH YOUR LAWYERS

Very little thought is given to how a person should deal with his lawyer. The lack of a planned relationship with your legal counsel can be a costly mistake. Your ability to get the most help at the least cost from your lawyers will depend on how well you communicate with them.

Your lawyers can be the source of intelligent advice and counsel or they can be merely legal rubber stamps, reflecting your own thoughts and ideas. Your lawyers can and should be the devil's advocates. If your deal will not stand up to searching questions, your deal may not be as good as it should be.

HELP YOUR LAWYERS HELP YOU

After you have located your lawyers, set up a procedure for working with him. The following list will prove helpful.

1. Don't bypass your lawyer; consult him first and last in each major deal.
2. Don't waste his time and your money in idle conversation. Prepare your points and your questions in advance.
3. Do your own personal research, then tell your lawyer your source of information.
4. Listen to your lawyer; hear and answer his questions.
5. Respect your lawyer's knowledge and experience.
6. Remember, your lawyer is for counsel and advice. You must still decide what you will do.
7. You, not your lawyer, are legally responsible for your actions.
8. It's your project, your money, and he's your lawyer. You should always remain in respectful control.

USE THE PROCEDURE

The reason for a detailed method of dealing with your legal counsel is simply to get better, more efficient legal assistance. Here, as usual, the most effective and efficient way is the least expensive.

Keep these facts dominant in your mind. No one knows your deals as well as you. No one cares about your deals as much as you. No one has to pay the bills and the taxes on your deals except you. DO NOT DEPEND ON ANYONE ELSE TO KNOW AND PROTECT YOUR INTERESTS.

Your attorneys, if properly selected, will have your best interest at heart. They can and will save you money and problems. They will do this if they know what the problems are. It is your

responsibility to keep your lawyers informed of your actions. It is
up to you to get legal advice before you act. You must be the one
to decide when to consult your lawyer.

REFERENCE BOOKS ARE MONEY IN THE BANK

In my library I have a number of books on law. Some of these
books are specifically on real estate law, and others are on business
and individual law. I also have current reference material on tax
laws.

I use these books to help me help my lawyers. I save my lawyers
many hours of searching for the proper legal references. When I
am working on a certain type real estate deal, I look up and read
all the data I can find on that type deal. I can then make an
outline of what I want to do and what I think is legal to do.

I submit this outline to my lawyers. I name my reference
sources. I tell them here is what I think I can do, now tell me if I
can do it. I also say, if their answer is negative, to explain why I
can't do it.

LAWYERS ARE NEGATIVE

When I make the statement lawyers are negative, I really mean
lawyers must look for the "no you can't" as well as the "yes you
can." Lawyers must look for the negative factors in any proposed
business deal.

In real estate, your lawyer must look for all types of possible
and actual legal problems. He will look for anything, such as a
mechanics lien, an error in wording of the title description—
anything that could put a legal cloud on the title. Your lawyer is
doing his job when he points out the negative factors.

LISTEN, THEN DECIDE

After you have presented your outline, after your lawyer has
studied the plan from the legal angle, then arrange a meeting with
your lawyer. At this meeting be prepared to listen. Don't be so

eager to do as you please that you do not hear the advice you are paying for.

Be the attentive audience, ask direct questions, listen to the answers, and consider all aspects of your plan. Weigh the negative side against the positive. Now it is time for you to make the final decision.

USE A CHECKLIST

1. Do you know your product
2. Have you made the Where, When, Why to buy decision
3. Are you buying the land right
4. Have you considered an option, a trade, co-ownership
5. Is the zoning suitable for your plan
6. Can the seller deliver a clear title
7. Have you considered the tax situation
8. Have you had the proposed contracts or legal documents checked
9. Do you have a plan for converting the land to a profit
10. Are you satisfied that this is the deal you will enjoy

If in your own mind you can answer the above checklist of questions in the affirmative—go.

No deal is perfect; you must take certain calculated risks. Use the checklist; use your own knowledge; consider the advice of others—then YOU DECIDE.

YOU CAN'T WAIT FOREVER

If you wait for the perfect deal, if you wait for all the factors to be just right, if you keep looking for a deal that is just a little better, just a little safer, just a little more of something, you may wait forever.

A medium profit from a medium deal is better than no profit while you look for that one in a million perfect deal. Study, plan, test, and deal. You can't profit as a dealer in land unless you deal in land.

Use your lawyer, your banker, and any other source for assistance in making the best possible decision. It is, however, up to you to make that final move, to say yes I will make that deal. Once you have made that first decision based on the method, then you can say with pride, "I am a dealer in land." It will almost surely follow that your income and your reputation will increase.

PERSONAL LEGAL PROTECTION

We have been examining the use of your lawyers to help you decide on a specific deal in land. Now we will consider another very important reason for legal assistance. Your lawyer should at all times look at each deal from the personal liability standpoint. You must have all the protection possible from any form of lawsuit. You will hold title to land; this can open up possibilities of a person being hurt on your land. Here you can protect yourself with liability insurance.

All legal documents used in contracting for land, improvements, etc., are subject to enforcement at law. The forms you used to sell the land must conform to certain well defined, and sometimes not so well defined, rules and laws.

The procedures you use, the methods of obtaining sales, can all be a source of legal problems. New laws come into existence, old laws are changed and even abolished. Only by working with legal counsel that is expert in the fields of real estate and taxes can you be protected. Only through the use of expert legal aid can you meet the legal requirements of your specific land deals.

PEACE OF MIND

The law is less rigid than most people realize. It has been the experience of the author that in legal matters the intent is very important. If, for example, a person deliberately and knowingly breaks a law, the punishment is often severe. If a person breaks a law that is unknown to him, he is still liable under that law; however, he can be almost certain of understanding treatment.

You are dealing in land to obtain profit and to enjoy that profit. You will only accomplish these goals if your deal is legal. You, working with your legal counsel, will be able to know and comply with the law. This is the path to peace of mind for the dealer in land.

USE THE CUSTOMER'S LAWYER

Many times when you are consummating a sale the buyer will want legal counsel. I have found that the land dealer should readily agree to this request. Do not use your lawyer; it is not proper legally or ethically for a lawyer to represent both parties in a transaction.

Have the buyer obtain his own lawyer. Make it clear that you will not pay any of the costs of such legal counsel. It is possible that you will on occasion lose a sale as a result of the buyer's lawyer. This is especially true where the sale is being made using a contract for deed. Some lawyers will not recommend that their client buy using such a contract.

In most cases the use by the buyer of his lawyer will only confirm the fact that you are offering a legitimate deal. This will reassure the buyer and he will enter into the agreement without the doubts he might have without legal guidance.

LEGAL TAX AVOIDANCE

The tax laws, whether income tax or others, are not as complicated as is generally believed. If you take your specific set of circumstances, if you study the tax laws relating just to your deals, you will be able to eliminate many of your tax problems.

Here you will start using your second lawyer. Here you use the expert in tax matters in much the same manner as the real estate lawyer. You must again help your tax lawyer to help you. You must furnish the facts, the plan. Only with complete knowledge of you and your deal can your tax attorney give you the best advice.

FIRST YOU

Make a complete case history of yourself. To do this, fill in the blanks in the following questionnaire:

Your Name _____ Address_____

Zip Code _____ Telephone (Home) ___ Telephone (Business)_____

Age _____ Number of Dependents_____

Place of Employment_____

Title _____ Annual Income _____ other income,
amount and source_____

_____

Wife's Name _____is she employed _____
if yes, where _____how long_____
annual income _____

ASSETS

Cash on Hand & In Banks . . . . $ _____
Savings Account in Banks . . . .   _____
U.S. Govt. Bonds . . . .   _____
Accts. & Notes Receivable . . . .   _____
Life Ins.–Cash Surrender Value Only . .   _____
Other Stocks and Bonds . . . .   _____
                (Describe on reverse side)
Real Estate . . . .   _____
                (Describe on reverse side)
Automobile–Present Value . . . .   _____
Other Personal Property . . . .   _____
                (Describe on reverse side)
Other Assets . . . .   _____
                (Describe on reverse side)
        TOTAL . . . . $ _____

LIABILITIES

Accounts Payable . . . .$ _____
Notes payable to Banks . . . .   _____
                        (Describe)
Notes Payable to Others . . . .   _____
                        (Describe)
Installment Acct. (Auto) . . . .   _____
                Monthly Payments $ _____   _____
Installment Accts. (Other) . . . .   _____
                Monthly Payments $ _____   _____
Loans on Life Insurance . . . .   _____
Mortgages on Real Estate . . . .   _____
                (Describe on reverse side)
Unpaid Taxes . . . .   _____
                (Describe on reverse side)
Other Liabilities . . . .   _____
                (Describe on reverse side)
Total Liabilities . . . .   _____
Net Worth . . . .   _____
        TOTAL . . . . $ _____

With the information from this form, plus your planned land program, your tax attorney can make intelligent recommendations.

As an example, your age is very important. It is obvious that the young man, newly married and just starting a family, has a completely different set of needs than the older man who has his family raised. In between these two we find the multitude of varying ages, problems, plans and desires.

TELL YOUR LAWYER ALL

Why anyone feels it is necessary to lie to his attorney is a mystery, yet according to many lawyers this is a serious problem. They claim that many clients either conceal or alter vital facts, thus giving the attorney the wrong information. Such altering of the facts can only result in the client receiving the wrong answers. You can't get the right answer from the wrong facts.

Tell your lawyer the facts; tell him all of the facts. Do this and you have the best chance of receiving the advice and counsel that will be right for you. Help your lawyer help you. Keep in mind that he is bound by a code of ethics. If you have used reasonable care in selecting your lawyer, you can give him your complete trust. If you ever find that any attorney breaches this trust, you should report him to the local Bar Association.

FACTS BRING RECOMMENDATIONS

From the facts you supply, your tax attorney will make certain recommendations. What action you take regarding these recommendations is for you to decide. Your attorney is not infallible; he can be wrong. You and you alone must decide on the course you will follow.

Keep this thought in mind: your tax lawyer has more experience and more knowledge in the tax field than you. It has been the author's experience that he goes against his real estate lawyer's advice much more than he goes against his tax lawyer's advice. The reason this is true is that the tax attorney has more definite laws covering tax matters.

In tax matters, the legal situation is generally the main concern.

In real estate matters, it is also the decision of even if it is legal, will it be profitable. In general, the real estate lawyer is dealing in more areas of opinion than the tax attorney.

We now find ourselves proving the need for expert help. To make a profit and then to keep as much of that profit as possible requires expert guidance. We live in a world where knowledge is the key to success. Couple your knowledge with that of your two attorneys and your percentage of right decisions will be very high.

YOU PAY TAXES ON PROFIT

To avoid income taxes, avoid profit. Yet, we are dealing in land to make a profit. How, then, can we consider that it is beneficial to avoid profits?

Income tax is computed on the amount of taxable income derived in a twelve month period. This is true of both personal and corporate tax. A corporation can have a tax year that does not begin on January 1st.

To control your tax liability, either personal or corporate, you must control your taxable income. This taxable income is, of course, based on the profit derived by you or your corporation. Now we will use an example of how your tax attorney can save you money if he has all of the facts.

You are operating as a dealer in land as an individual. Your taxable income from your regular job is $10,000 per year. Based on such taxable income and your marital and family situation, you will pay 30 percent of the $10,000 in federal and state income taxes. In money, you will pay $3,000. Now add income from your spare time land deal. We will use for an example a $5,000 profit from a cash sale in land.

We add the $5,000 land profits to the $10,000 taxable income from your regular job. You now have a taxable income of $15,000. The rate on this for you will be 45 percent, and computed in dollars you will pay $6,750 in income tax. This leaves you $8,250 in actual spendable income after taxes.

HOW TO AVOID THE HIGH TAX BRACKET

You could have avoided a great deal of the extra tax by selling the land on terms. Here is how the terms sale would work.

Your regular taxable income	$10,000
Sale of land with 20 percent down	
Payable in five years, results	
in a first year taxable income of	$ 1,000
Total taxable income based on $10,000 salary	$11,000
Your tax rate 35 percent of your tax liability is	$ 3,850

This results in your paying $2,900 less taxes than if you had sold the land on a cash basis. Paying $2,900 for the $4,000 cash in the same tax year would have resulted in only $1,100 of additional spendable income.

Based on your regular taxable income remaining at approximately the same level, you will have an after tax spendable income from the land sale of $650 per year for the next four years, plus additional income from the interest payments.

Here you have deferred profit and increased spendable income. You are obligated to pay less income tax, and you added income from the interest you received.

This is only an example: the amounts and percentages are reasonably correct. The absolute fact is that you normally pay income tax only on profit or income received in a twelve month tax period. Your tax attorney can tell you how to comply with the tax regulations as to taxes relating to land sales on payments. Special note: To arrive at the taxable profit on a land deal, you deduct the following: land cost, cost of any improvements, sales and advertising expense, travel and personal expense related to the purchase and sale of the land, fees, taxes, interest, and other costs relative to the total deal.

Only after these deductions do you arrive at your taxable income. It is also possible that you may be able to deal on a small scale in land and pay income tax based on long term capital gains.

CONSULT YOUR ATTORNEY

Please, do not be your own lawyer. Check each deal carefully with your legal counsel. Follow the procedure outlined in this chapter. Help your lawyers help you.

There are many ways to use land to build your estate without incurring a tax liability. If you use your tax lawyer, if you plan ahead, you can accumulate a fortune in land and never pay any income tax.

A MILLION DOLLAR NET WORTH WITH NO INCOME TAX

You do not pay income tax on land appreciation as your land holdings become more valuable. As time and circumstances combine to increase your net worth in land, you are not required to pay any income tax on that increase. Appreciation in land value is not subject to income tax until you take it in cash or equivalent.

Your estate can increase from a thousand dollars to one hundred thousand dollars and you would not pay one dime in income taxes. You could even borrow ten to fifty thousand dollars on this land value and still not owe any income tax.

Under existing tax laws at the time of this writing, you in fact would now have two sources of tax deductions. You could legally deduct the property taxes on the land and also deduct the interest you pay on the loan.

Believe it or not, you could make a MILLION DOLLARS in appreciated net worth dealing in land and not pay any income tax.

POINTS WHERE INCOME TAX LAWS MAKE DEALS

1. Landowner may be able to get capital gains treatment only if he sells you all his land at one time.
2. Landowner may reduce his tax substantially be selling to you on terms.
3. Landowner participation may increase his income without proportionately increasing his income taxes.
4. Landowner may be able to trade land for land with you, and neither of you have any tax liability.
5. Landowner can defer tax liability by giving you an option or conditional contract.
6. Landowner can borrow on the installment contract used to sell you the land. In this manner he can receive a substantial amount of cash. There should be no income tax liability on the cash from such a loan.

CHECK WITH YOUR LAWYER

In this chapter we have discussed and used examples of why two lawyers, and how to help your lawyer. We have considered personal liability and peace of mind by being legally correct. We have covered a very tiny portion of the tax situation in dealing in land. We have said a little about many things; we have only touched the surface of LAWS AND TAXES.

Please use this chapter only as a guide to the source of legal knowledge. DO NOT USE ANY PART OF THIS CHAPTER WITHOUT SPECIFIC LEGAL ADVICE FROM YOUR ATTORNEY.

This chapter has only given you a layman's view of real estate law. It has endeavored to answer various problems that arise in dealing in land. I recommend that any serious reader of this book should have in his library Robert W. Semenow's book, *Questions and Answers on Real Estate,* published by Prentice-Hall, Inc. It contains in detail the answers to almost any legal or technical real estate problem. Another excellent book in this area is *Real Estate Law* by Robert Kratovil, also published by Prentice-Hall, Inc.

9

Protecting Your Profits with the Right Documents

To properly use the various documents necessary to deal in land, you must have certain knowledge. You must, for example, know what laws govern land transactions. You must know what land is, and what it contains. You need to know if you always receive all of the use and benefits of the land you buy. Can you, for instance, sell various rights to the land in separate sales to different buyers?

What is real property? What is a chattel? These and many more questions must be answered before you can understand when and how to use the proper documents. This chapter will help you learn the basics.

LAND AND THE LAW

Land is subject to many and diverse laws. Federal laws governing land are basically uniform in all the states of the union. State land laws vary to such a degree that you must consider each land deal based on the states involved. All laws are subject to revision and change. You must always use current references to the law—yesterday's truth may be today's error. Check the current legal situation before you complete your land deal.

DEFINITION OF LAND

Land is the soil and its contents, which includes trees, grass, shrubs, minerals, oil, gas, etc. With the purchase of land you normally obtain all of these, plus the air rights. We will now examine if we always receive all of the use and benefits of the land we purchase.

We have defined land as the soil, its contents, and the air space above it. It is possible and legal to sell land content separate from the land—these sales may be to separate buyers. The owner of land can sell the grass as sod, the trees as timber, the shrubs as decorations, the minerals, oil and gas for extraction. The owner can sell all of these and still own and have the legal right to sell the land as a separate entity.

If such sales have been made, it is the duty of the seller to make these facts known to the buyer. The details of such prior sales or assignments must appear in writing in the title conveyance.

MONEY FROM LAND YOU DON'T OWN

The owner of land can sell soil content rights and then subsequently sell the land minus these rights. In plain terms, the land owner can deliver legal title to the land and still retain in perpetutity the mineral, gas and oil rights. The author has a business associate who can be cited as an example of profits from land you don't own, in this case profits from land that was never owned by this man.

This associate of mine is receiving a substantial annual income from gas and oil leases he inherited. One of his relatives owned land; this relative sold the land and retained the mineral, gas and oil rights. These rights were assigned for an annual fee to an oil company.

This relative died, and the leases and the rights passed with his estate to the parents of my associate. Upon the death of the parents, these rights passed to my associate. Here is income being received from land that was sold many years ago. This income can continue for many years to come. If oil is discovered on this land, all of the income would come not to the land owner, but to the person holding the oil rights.

You can buy and sell land with or without the use or control of all of its elements. This fact can be a great help to you in making profitable land deals. Knowing what you are buying or selling and how to protect your interests is a major profit principle in dealing in land.

AIR RIGHTS

With the purchase of land, you normally receive the air space rights. This is the right to the control and use of the air space directly above your land. An example of this right is a gate on your neighbor's land that swings across your land. Even though this gate does not touch your land, it trespasses on your air space and is therefore illegal. You can stop this trespass by legal means and force your neighbor to cease the act of trespassing.

This air space right can be sold as a separate sale from the actual sale of the land. In some cities, railway tracks are below the normal level of the surrounding land. The use by modern trains is such that the owners of this land can and do sell the air space rights, starting a certain number of feet above the tracks. This air space is used to construct multi-storied buildings. This allows the railway to continue its normal use of the land and still gain income from the lease or sale of the air space.

REAL PROPERTY

Real Property or realty is land, including all the elements described in the land definition plus any buildings that may be on the land at the time of sale. When title is conveyed to a certain piece of land, that title includes all the elements of the soil, the air space above the land, and all of the buildings thereon—unless they are specifically exempted in writing in the deed.

When title to a piece of land is conveyed, the buyer normally receives all the real property involved.

CHATTEL

There are numerous items that may be on the land or in the buildings that do not go with the land. These items are generally referred to as chattels. Chattels may be simply defined as those items not permanently affixed to or a part of the land or the buildings.

All furniture that is not built-in is chattel. In the purchase of realty, you should never expect to receive title to chattels. It is best to have items of this nature that are to be included in the sale listed in the sale contract. With such a list, both parties know what items go with the sale.

NOW YOU KNOW WHAT, NOW LEARN HOW

You have just studied the basics of what land is and what it contains. You have found that realty is one thing and chattels another. You have been warned that you may or may not receive all of the benefits of realty when you buy. You have also discovered that you can sell elements of the land in separate profitable sales. Now you will study how to actually consummate these deals and what documents to use. We will start with how to give and receive title to realty.

A DEED IS A CONTRACT

Because in effect a deed is a contract, a deed must contain the elements of a contract. In general and always subject to current federal and state law, a deed should contain the following information.

BASICS OF A DEED

1. Date—this is to establish a basis of time. In general, the date of actual delivery of the deed to the buyer is the legal date of conveyance.
2. Names and addresses—of the persons granting and of the

persons receiving title. Full names including middle name or initial should be used.

3. The consideration—this can in most cases be stated as good or valuable consideration. Insert the following "and one dollar." It is not necessary to state the actual or true consideration.

4. Grant and convey—this is used to state that the seller does grant and convey the ownership of the following described land.

5. Location of the land—this includes the county, the state, and a legal description of the lots, tracts, or parcels of land.

6. Easements and restrictions—we must be certain that the person receiving title is aware of existing easements and restrictions of record.

7. Special notations—regarding such factors as mineral, gas and oil rights not being included. If any of the normal rights to the land has already been sold, such facts should be clearly stated.

8. Seller warrants that he has the right to convey title free and clear of liens and encumbrances. He further warrants that he will defend title to the land.

9. The deed must be signed by the seller and in most cases by his spouse. Exception to the requirement of the seller's signature is the use of Power of Attorney. In some states the signature must be witnessed and in some states it must be sealed. A corporate deed must have the corporate seal affixed. A corporate deed in most cases must be signed by a corporate officer, president or vice-president, and the secretary or assistant secretary.

10. In addition to the signing, sealing and witnessing that may be required, it is a general condition for the seller to formally declare the sale in front of a Notary Public or like official. This official then affirms the signature of the seller.

11. Delivery is the final legal act of transfer of title. A deed can be considered delivered without the buyer actually touching the deed. A deed can be delivered by words as well as act.

DELIVERY THROUGH ESCROW

When for special reasons a third party is brought into the delivery of the title to land, we have the following situation. The seller agrees to deliver title if certain monies are deposited with the third party (generally a bank); the buyer agrees that on or prior to a certain date he will deposit the required money with the third party. A deed is drawn and signed by the seller. The deed is given to the third party, with instructions on the basis of the delivery requirements.

When the buyer completes his part of the agreement, the third party delivers the deed to the buyer. In the event the buyer does not complete his part of the agreement, the deed is returned to the seller.

The use of the third party can also be used to allow the buyer the opportunity to check the title before paying the purchase money. Any time there is a need for a deed to be delivered upon completion of certain conditions, the delivery can be made using a third party.

RECORDING

When the buyer has received delivery of the deed, he has legal title to the land. The knowledge of this title to the land is known by only a few persons. To protect his position as the legal owner of this land, the buyer is required to record his deed.

This act of recording is in most cases simple, and the fee is nominal. It is therefore strange that this last act of ownership is the one most generally not done by the buyer. The author of this book has deeded thousands of lots and tracts of land to excited, happy buyers. I have had numbers of them hold their deeds unrecorded for years.

Until your deed is recorded, there is no public legal record of your ownership of the land. If by error or dishonest design the original owner should issue another deed to the same land and the buyer recorded his deed, he would become the owner of record. Your immediate recording of the deed may well save you legal problems. Do not delay in this final but crucial act in the purchase of land.

TYPES OF DEEDS

Warranty Deed

A warranty deed claims in writing that the seller can convey the land and give a good title free and clear of any encumbrances. It further claims that the seller will defend the buyer forever against lawful claims and demands of all persons whomsoever. (See Exhibit 9-1.)

Special Warranty Deed

Similar to a regular warranty deed with this exception, "the seller restricts his liability for encumbrances prior to his ownership." (See Exhibit 9-2.)

Deeds of Bargain and Sale

As long as a deed contains the proper information as to consideration, land description and conveyance, it is a deed of Bargain and Sale. A deed of bargain and sale that includes warranty of title is a warranty deed as described above.

Quit-Claim Deed

A quit-claim deed is generally used to remove a possible interest or a possible partial interest in the title to a piece of real property. The quit-claim deed is used as the instrument to assure that such possible interests do not constitute a cloud on the title. (See Exhibit 9-3.)

Deed in Blank

There are times when the owner of land will issue a deed that is complete in all but one respect. Such a deed will omit the name and address of the person who is to receive title to the land. This deed is called a deed in blank. There are two main reasons for the use of a deed in blank.

1. The deed in blank is given to an agent with instructions to sell the land at a stipulated price. When the agent has found a buyer at the agreed price, he inserts the buyer's name in the deed and makes delivery.

2. The deed in blank is used as collateral on a loan. The deed in blank is part of the collateral for a loan obtained by the seller on a contract for deed for the land described in the blank deed.

FORM NO. 2 CLASS E   DEMAREE STATIONERY CO., 908 Walnut, Kansas City, Mo.

Missouri Warranty Deed

This Indenture, *Made on the*   *day of*   *A. D., One*

Thousand Nine Hundred and   *by and between*

of the County of   *, State of*   *part*   *of the first part, and*

of the County of   *, State of*   *part*   *of the second part.*

(Mailing address of said first named grantee is   *).*

WITNESSETH: THAT THE SAID PART   *OF THE FIRST PART,* in consideration of the

sum of   *DOLLARS*

to   *paid by said part*   *of the second part (the receipt of which is hereby acknowledged), do*

by these presents, Grant, Bargain and Sell, Convey and Confirm unto the said part   *of the second*

part   *heirs and assigns, the following described lots, tracts or parcels of land*

lying, being and situate in the County of   *and State of Missouri, to-wit:*

*TO HAVE AND TO HOLD The premises aforesaid with all and singular, the rights, privileges, appur-
tenances and immunities thereto belonging or in any wise appertaining unto the said part*   *of the
second part and unto*   *heirs and assigns forever; the said*
hereby covenanting that
lawfully seized of an indefeasible estate in fee of the premises herein conveyed; that   *ha
good right to convey the same; that the said premises are free and clear from any incumbrance done or suffered
by*   *or those under whom*   *claim   ; and that   will
warrant and defend the title to the said premises unto the said part*   *of the second part and unto*
heirs and assigns forever, against the lawful claims and demands of all persons
whomsoever

IN WITNESS WHEREOF, The said part   *of the first part ha   hereunto set
hand   and seal   the day and year above written.*

(SEAL)

(SEAL)

(SEAL)

(SEAL)

Courtesy of Demaree Stationery Company, 908 Walnut, Kansas City, Missouri

Exhibit 9-1. Warranty Deed

MISSOURI ACKNOWLEDGMENT—UNMARRIED PERSON

STATE OF..
} ss.
COUNTY OF...

On this...................day of.........................., 19.......

before me, ..., a Notary Public, personally appeared

to me known to be the person described in and who executed the foregoing instrument, and acknowledged that.........................
executed the same as..................................free act and deed. And the said ....
further declare...to be single and unmarried.

IN WITNESS WHEREOF, I have hereunto set my hand and affixed my official seal at
my office in...the day and year last above written.

My term expires.., 19........   Notary Public in and for said County and State.

MISSOURI ACKNOWLEDGMENT—MAN AND WIFE

STATE OF..
} ss.
COUNTY OF...

On this...................day of.........................., 19.......

before me, ..., a Notary Public, personally appeared

....and...
his wife, to me known to be the persons described in and who executed the foregoing instrument, and acknowledged
that they executed the same as their free act and deed.

IN TESTIMONY WHEREOF, I have hereunto set my hand and affixed my official seal at
my office in...the day and year last above written.

My term expires.., 19........   Notary Public in and for said County and State.

Warranty Deed

FROM

TO

Filed for record this.............day
of.........................A.D., 19.......
at............o'clock............minutes,............M.
Recorded in Book............at Page............
Recorder.
By............Deputy.
Recorder's Fee, $............

STATE OF..
} ss.
COUNTY OF...

IN THE RECORDER'S OFFICE

I,.., Recorder of said County, do hereby certify that the within
instrument of writing was. at............o'clock and............minutes............M., on the ....day of............
A. D., 19......., duly filed for record in my office, and is recorded in the records of this office, in book............, at page............
IN WITNESS WHEREOF, I have hereunto set my hand and affixed my official seal at............
this............day of.........................   A. D., 19.......

....Recorder.

Courtesy of Demaree Stationery Company, 908 Walnut, Kansas City, Missouri

Exhibit 9-1. Warranty Deed (Continued)

SPECIAL WARRANTY DEED

THIS INDENTURE, Made on the_____ day of _____19___,
by and between _____, a Missouri corporation
of the County of Jackson, State of Missouri, First Party,
and
            Name and Address of buyer

of the County of   , State of   ,
Second Part

WITNESSETH, That the said First Party, in consideration
of the sum of Ten Dollars ($10.00) and other good and
valuable considerations, to it paid by the said Second Part
(the receipt of which is hereby acknowledged) does by these
presents, sell and convey unto the said Second Part   ,
heirs and assigns, the following described lots, tracts or
parcels of land, lying, being and situated in the County of
Stone and State of Missouri, to-wit:

            Description of property

TO HAVE AND TO HOLD The premises aforesaid, with all and
singular the rights, privileges, appurtenances and immunities
Second Part   , and unto   heirs and assigns forever the
said _____, hereby covenanting that the
said premises are free and clear from any incumbrance done
or suffered by it and that it will warrant and defend the
title to said premises unto the said Second Part   and unto
      heirs and assigns forever, against the lawful claims
and demands of all persons claiming under it.

IN WITNESS WHEREOF, The said First Party has caused
these presents to be signed by its President and attested
by its Secretary, and the corporate seal to be hereunto
attached the day and year first above written.

Attest: By_____

_____
      Secretary

Courtesy of Kirk C. Colony of Ozarks, Inc., Kansas City, Missouri

Exhibit 9-2. Special Warranty Deed

FORM NO. 16—CLASS E

DEMAREE STATIONERY CO., 908 Walnut, Kansas City, Mo.

Quit-Claim Deed

This Indenture, Made on the   day of   A. D., One
Thousand Nine Hundred and   by and between

of the County of   , State of   part of the first part, and

of the County of   , State of   part of the second part.
(Mailing address of said first named grantee is   ).

WITNESSETH, that the said part   of the first part, in consideration of the sum of

DOLLARS,

to   paid by the said part   of the second part (the receipt of which is hereby acknowledged)

do   by these presents REMISE, RELEASE and FOREVER QUIT CLAIM unto the said part

of the second part, the following described lots, tracts or parcels of land, lying, being and situate in the

County of   and State of   , to-wit:

TO HAVE AND TO HOLD THE SAME, with all the rights, immunities, privileges and appurtenances thereto belonging, unto the said part   of the second part and unto   heirs and
assigns forever; so that neither the said part   of the first part nor   heirs nor any other
person or persons, for   or in   name or behalf, shall or will hereinafter
claim or demand any right or title to the aforesaid premises or any part thereof, but they and each of
them shall, by these presents, be excluded and forever barred.

IN WITNESS WHEREOF, the said part   of the first part ha   hereunto set
hand   and seal   the day and year above written.

_____(Seal)

Signed, Sealed and Delivered in Presence of   _____(Seal)

_____   _____(Seal)

_____   _____(Seal)

Courtesy of Demaree Stationery Company, 908 Walnut, Kansas City, Missouri

Exhibit 9-3. Quit-Claim Deed

MISSOURI ACKNOWLEDGMENT—UNMARRIED PERSON

STATE OF ....
COUNTY OF .... } ss.   On this..............................day of............................., 19.......

before me,.. a Notary Public, personally appeared

....
to me known to be the person described in and who executed the foregoing instrument, and acknowledges that............................
executed the same as...free act and deed. And the said...
further declare..to be single and unmarried.
IN TESTIMONY WHEREOF, I have hereunto set my hand and affixed my official seal at my
office in...the day and year last above written.

My term expires......................................., 19. ...   Notary Public in and for said County and State.

MISSOURI ACKNOWLEDGMENT—MAN AND WIFE

STATE OF ....
COUNTY OF .... } ss.   On this......................day of........................, 19.......

before me,..a Notary Public, personally appeared

....and..
his wife, to me known to be the persons described in and who executed the foregoing instrument, and acknowledged that they
executed the same as their free act and deed.
IN TESTIMONY WHEREOF, I have hereunto set my hand and affixed my official seal at my
office in...the day and year last above written.

My term expires......................................., 19. ...   Notary Public in and for said County and State

STATE OF...
COUNTY OF... } ss.   IN THE RECORDER'S OFFICE

I, ..., Recorder of said County, do hereby certify that the within
instrument of writing was, at...................o'clock and.................minutes.........M., on the...........day of...........................
A.D., 19......., duly filed for record in my office, and is recorded in the records of this office, in book..............., at page...............
IN WITNESS WHEREOF, I have hereunto set my hand and affixed my official seal at......................................
this................day of...........................A. D., 19......

....Recorder.

Courtesy of Demaree Stationery Company, 908 Walnut, Kansas City, Missouri

Exhibit 9-3. Quit-Claim Deed (Continued)

Deeds with Special Stipulations

When land is sold under special circumstances, these circumstances must be explained in the deed. An example of special circumstances would be the prior assignment or sale of the mineral rights of the land being deeded.

RESTRICTIONS

Restrictions are a covenant between the seller and the buyer as to the necessity for doing certain things or the prohibition of doing certain things. An example of a restriction would be that the buyer of a certain lot in a certain sub-division could not use that lot for commercial purposes. The seller could sell the lot adjacent to such restricted lot and not include such a restriction. In simple terms, the owner of a sub-division is not required to have the same restrictions on all the lots in the sub-division.

Restrictions may appear written in the deed or may be on a separate instrument. When the restrictions are on a separate instrument, this instrument should be of record and it must be referred to in the deed.

Restrictions should be written in a careful but simple manner. They must be clear as to intent. They should in themselves be legal. If a given restriction is declared illegal, such declaration would have no effect on the other restrictions. The remaining restrictions would remain in full force. Restrictions travel with the title to the land and all subsequent owners. For the time period of the restrictions, all owners are bound by these restrictions. (See Exhibit 9-4.)

EASEMENTS

Easements are the giving of rights of use of a portion of the land to another party. This use is in general dealing with uses that in themselves do not profit the user in a material sense. An example of such easement is the allowing of utility lines to cross a property so that all property owners may obtain these utilities.

You may write an easement into a deed for many reasons: as

BUILDING LIMITATIONS AND RESTRICTIONS: CLUB MANOR ESTATES
                                         PALO DURO X, MIRAMAR ESTATES

Now, THEREFORE, said Proprietors hereby declare that said protective restrictions are
hereby imposed on said protective area and are as follows to-wit:

1. That the Grantee or Grantees, under conveyance, shall not at any time conduct,
   or permit to be conducted on said premises, any trade or business of any description,
   nor shall said premises be used for any other purpose whatsoever except for the purpose of a private dwelling or residence and normal recreational purposes.

2. No building shall be erected or any improvement of any kind shall be erected, moved
   on to, or maintained on the premises herein described until the design and location
   therefore has first been submitted to and approved by Proprietors or their assigns.

3. No building shall be erected in said subdivision on anything but a permanent con-
   crete or masonry type footing, piers, or foundation.

4. No building shall have any other exterior finish than stone, stucco, brick, stained
   or painted wood or shingles. In no case shall a roll type asphalt siding be
   considered as acceptable.

5. No building intended for human habitation shall have any other type roof than cedar,
   built up roof with gravel surface or composition roofing, and no roof shall have a
   roll roof.

6. No cottage constructed in Club Manor Estates shall have less than an outside
   dimension of 20' X 24'.

7. No trailer, tent, shack, garage or other outbuildings shall at any time be used as
   a residence temporarily or permanently, except with the special written permission
   from the undersigned Proprietors or their assigns for use during construction of
   cottage.

8. The construction of any building shall be completed and ready for occupancy within
   18 months after that construction is started on said building.

9. All residential buildings constructed upon said lots shall have modern sanitary
   facilities and in no case shall outdoor toilets be constructed upon said lots.

10. Each dwelling and other permitted accessory buildings shall occupy at least one full
    lot as shown on the recorded plat, and under no circumstances shall two or more
    dwellings be erected on a single lot.

11. A permanent easement is hereby reserved along, over and under 10 feet of the rear
    lot line of each lot for the purpose of providing access and use by public utilities,
    drainage lines, sewers, etc.

12. No noxious or offensive activity shall be carried on upon any lot, nor shall anything
    be done thereon which may be, or may become an annoyance, or nuisance to the neigh-
    borhood, nor shall any refuse be so disposed of as to create a nuisance, filth, or
    unsightly condition. PROPERTY OWNERS SHALL KEEP THEIR PROPERTY FREE FROM WEEDS AND
    BRUSH. All trash and rubbish shall be immediately removed from the premise and no
    unsightly objects shall be left on the premises, but shall be disposed of in areas
    provided for that purpose.

13. No animals, livestock, or poultry of any kind shall be raised, bred, or kept on any
    lot, except that dogs, cats, or other hosehold pets may be kept provided that they
    are not kept, bred, or maintained for any commercial purpose.

14. Nothing contained in this declaration shall impair or defeat the lien of any mortgage
    or deed of trust made in good faith and for value, but titles to any property
    subject to this declaration obtained through sale in satisfaction of any such
    mortgage or deed of trust shall thereafter be held subject to all the protective
    restrictions hereof.

15. That each and all of the protective restrictions shall be enforceable by injunction
    or any other form of action available to the parties aggrieved, or to the Corpa-
    tion or its successors in interest. Invalidation of any of these protective
    restrictions by judgment or court order shall in no wise affect any other provision,
    which shall remain in full force and effect.

I (We) have read, understand and agree to the above restrictions.

                              _____(Purchaser)

Courtesy of Kirk C. Colony of Ozarks, Inc., Kansas City, Missouri

Exhibit 9-4. Building Limitations and Restrictions

mentioned before for utilities, for access to adjoining property as in the case of a path or roadway, and many others. There can be many types of written and implied easements. In general, the dealer in land will only be involved in utility and access easements.

DEED IN TRUST

A deed in trust is in effect a form of escrow. As we know, escrow is the use of a third party in a real estate transaction. In the case of the deed in trust method of handling a real estate sale or purchase, the following procedure is used.

An escrow agent, generally a bank or trust company, holds the sale contract and the deed to the property. The buyer makes his payment or payments to the escrow agent. Upon completion of the terms of the contract, the escrow agent delivers the deed to the buyer.

The use of the escrow agent is to protect the interests of both the buyer and the seller. If the agent involved is conversant with all of the details, he can and will fulfill this safeguard function. (Example of legal document used in one such land deal follows.)

CONTRACT FOR SALE OF REAL ESTATE AND
ESCROW AGREEMENT

This Agreement, made and entered into this _____ day of _____, 19___, by _____ of _____ County, Kansas, Buyers, _____ a _____ corporation, Seller, and _____ National Bank of _____, a national banking association, Escrow Agent.

WITNESSETH:

1. Seller hereby sells to Buyers, and Buyers hereby purchase from Seller, certain real property lying, being and situated in Stone County, Missouri, the legal description of which is set out in Exhibit "A".

2. Seller's warranty deed conveying all its right, title and interest in and to the subject property and naming Buyers as Grantees has this day been delivered to Escrow Agent, and Escrow Agent hereby acknowledges receipt of such deed.

3. The total purchase price for the subject property is Twenty-Five Thousand Dollars ($25,000) which Buyers agree to pay as follows:

(a) Buyers have previously paid Seller the sum of Five Hundred Dollars ($500) as partial consideration, and Seller hereby acknowledges the receipt of such sum.

(b) Buyers have this date paid Seller the sum of Four Thousand Five Hundred Dollars ($4,500) as additional partial consideration, and Seller hereby acknowledges the receipt of such sum.

(c) Buyers agree to pay the balance of the purchase price, Twenty Thousand Dollars ($20,000), in payments of principal and interest as follows:

(i) The sum of Two Thousand Five Hundred Twenty Dollars ($2,520) on April 15, 19___ and the like amount on each of the next eleven succeeding anniversary dates of such payment until principal and interest have been paid in full;

(ii) The unpaid balance of the purchase price will bear interest at the rate of seven (7) percent per annum, interest to accrue from April 15, 19___;

(iii) Buyers may prepay any part or all of the purchase price at any time and from time to time, without penalty, it being specifically agreed that prepayments must be clearly identified as such, and no prepayment shall relieve Buyers of the obligation to make the above described payments on April 15, 19___ and anniversary dates thereof;

(iv) All deferred payments will be made to Escrow Agent to be held or disposed of in accordance with the terms of this Agreement;

(v) Payments received by Escrow Agent shall be allocated first to interest accrued, and the balance allocated to payment of principal.

4. Escrow Agent agrees to accept and receive all deferred payments from Buyers. Escrow Agent shall distribute the full amount of such payments to Seller, promptly upon receipt thereof, provided; however, that Escrow Agent shall be entitled to an annual fee in the amount of _____ ($___) which Escrow Agent may deduct each year from receipts before making distributions; provided, further, that when the terms and provisions of this agreement direct that Seller deliver a deed or deeds to Escrow Agent for distribution to Buyers, Escrow Agent shall not make then current distributions until it receives such deed or deeds.

5. When Escrow Agent receives final payment of principal and interest, the escrow agreement hereby created shall terminate, and Escrow Agent shall forthwith deliver Seller's warranty deed then held in escrow to _____ or such other company as may be acceptable to Buyers, for inspection and recording. Seller agrees to furnish Buyers at the time of delivery of said deed a title policy issued by _____ insuring in Buyers for $25,000 a fee simple title in the subject land free and clear of all liens and encumbrances whatsoever except any liens or encumbrances approved by Buyers in writing provided however that the buyer shall not unreasonably fail to give

such approval, and Escrow Agent may deduct the amount of the premium for such policy from escrow funds before distributing the balance to Seller.

6. Attached hereto as Exhibit "B" is an unrecorded plat map (not an actual survey of the subject property) showing the subject property divided into seven (7) tracts designated Tract A through Tract G inclusive. Buyers shall be entitled to request and receive a deed or deeds to one or more of such tracts as follows:

(a) As a part of Exhibit "B", an amount is assigned to each tract which is a part of the subject property. In the event Buyers prepay part of the purchase price, and if the amount so prepaid, principal and interest, equals or exceeds the amount assigned to a particular tract or to particular tracts, Buyers may give written request to Escrow Agent, such request to accompany Buyer's prepayment, for delivery of Seller's deed or deeds to such tract or tracts. Buyers, in their request, shall specify the designation given such tract or tracts in Exhibit "B" and give a legal description, acceptable to Seller, of such tract or tracts. Escrow Agent shall notify Seller of such prepayment and request for deed, and Seller shall deliver the following deeds to Escrow Agent:

(i) Its warranty deed or deeds to the tract or tracts specified by Buyers conveying title of the quality specified in paragraph 5 hereof, such deed or deeds to be delivered to Buyers.

(ii) Its warranty deed for all the rest and remainder of the subject property to be retained in escrow. On delivery of such deeds, Escrow Agent shall make a distribution of escrow funds to Seller.

(b) In addition, when the outstanding principal balance of the purchase price has been reduced to Ten Thousand Dollars ($10,000), or less, Buyers may give written request to Escrow Agent for delivery of Seller's deed or deeds to any two of the tracts designated Tract A, Tract B, Tract C or Tract D in Exhibit "B", assuming same have not previously been deeded to Buyers as provided in paragraph (a) of this section 6. And, when the outstanding principal balance of the purchase price has been reduced to Five Thousand Dollars ($5,000) or less, Buyers may give written request to Escrow Agent for delivery of Seller's deed to either of the two tracts designated Tract E and Tract F, the choice to be that of Buyers, assuming same has not previously been deeded to Buyers as provided in paragraph (a) of this section 6. Buyers, in their request or requests, shall specify the designation given such tract or tracts in Exhibit "B" and give a legal description, acceptable to Seller, of such tract or tracts. Seller shall then deliver the following deeds to Escrow Agent:

(i) Its warranty deed or deeds to the tract or tracts specified by Buyers, conveying title of the quality specified in paragraph 5 hereof, such deed or deeds to be delivered to Buyers;

(ii) Its warranty deed for all the rest and remainder of the subject property to be retained in escrow.

(c) Attached hereto as Exhibit "C" is an unrecorded map of the subject property showing how same could be subdivided and showing the location of private roads and access ways across the subject property. Seller shall have free use of such private roads and access ways as shown in Exhibit "C" for ingress and egress to and from the subject property and any part thereof, Seller's rights to continue in perpetuity or until such times as Buyers acquire fee simple absolute title in and to all of the subject property; provided, however, the grant of rights herein shall apply only to such roads and ways as now exist and no obligation on Buyers to construct any additional roads and ways shall be implied.

7. Seller warrants that it has marketable title in and to the subject property and that its Board of Directors in a special meeting held on the ___ day of _____, 19___ approved the sale of the subject property and the form of this agreement and authorized the undersigned to execute this agreement for Seller. Seller covenants that all deeds which Escrow Agent, in accordance with its instructions as herein given, delivers to Buyers will, on such delivery, vest Buyers with unencumbered fee simple absolute title in and to that part or all of the subject property therein described.

8. Seller shall not be required to pay premiums for title insurance until principal and interest have been paid in full. If Buyers purchase title insurance on tracts of land for which they receive deeds prior to the delivery to Buyers of Seller's final deed, then on delivery of Seller's final deed, Escrow Agent will refund to Buyers an amount equal to that amount then charged by _____ for a Twenty Five Thousand Dollar ($25,000) title insurance policy; provided, however, that the amount so refunded shall not exceed the amount of premiums paid by Buyers.

9. Buyers will be deemed to be in default of their obligation to make stated payments on or before April 15 of each year during the term of this escrow arrangement if any one such payment has not been received by Escrow Agent by 12:01 A.M. on April 16. In the event of such default, the total principal balance then outstanding and accrued interest shall immediately become due and payable and such acceleration shall occur without notice of default or demand for cure to Buyers. Buyers hereby waiving presentment of notice and demand for cure. If Buyers fail to pay total principal balance outstanding at the time of such default and accrued interest within ninety (90) days after such written notice of default, Escrow Agent shall return any deed or deeds then held in escrow to Seller together with all escrow funds less any amount retained by Escrow Agent in payment of its fees, and all rights of Buyers in and to the land covered by the deed or deeds so returned to Seller will be deemed terminated. Acceptance by Escrow Agent, on instructions from Seller, of partial payment of principal and interest after Buyers' default shall not be deemed a waiver of any subsequent default. If Seller shall fail to deliver to Buyers title to the subject property of the quality described in paragraph 5 and the title insurance policy provided for in said paragraph 5 upon full performance

by Buyers of their obligations under this contract, Seller shall pay to Buyers within 30 days the entire amount paid by Buyers pursuant to this contract with interest at the rate of 7 percent per annum from the date of Seller's failure to so perform to the date of payment. Should Buyers be required to bring suit to enforce the foregoing covenant of Seller, Seller shall pay all expenses incurred by Buyers in enforcing such payment, including reasonable attorney fees.

10. Buyers agree that no amount in addition to interest on the deferred purchase price of Twenty Thousand Dollars ($20,000) has been added as a finance charge or other charge and that total deferred payments, if no amount is prepaid, which they will pay under the terms of this agreement will be Thirty Thousand Two Hundred Forty Dollars ($30,240) and that the annual percentage rate of interest charged is seven (7) percent.

11. Exhibit "A," Exhibit "B," and Exhibit "C," and Exhibit "D," each of which is attached hereto, are, by this reference and all other references in this agreement, incorporated herein and made a part hereof.

12. The terms and provisions of this agreement shall be binding upon and inure to the benefit of the parties hereto, their respective heirs, successors, assigns and personal representatives.

13. Buyers and Seller agree that Escrow Agent will not be required to perform any services or discharge any responsibilities in addition to those herein described, and Escrow Agent shall not be required to look beyond the terms of any deed or other instrument it receives hereunder.

IN WITNESS WHEREOF, the parties hereto have caused this agreement to be executed on the date and year first above written.

_____
_____
                                                                BUYERS
(Corporate Seal)   _____
ATTEST: By_____
                                                       President

_____
Secretary   SELLER

                                    _____NATIONAL BANK

(Corporate Seal)
ATTEST: By_____
                                              ESCROW AGENT

_____
Secretary

SALE BY DEED OF TRUST

A sale by deed of trust is similar in many respects to a sale by contract with the deed in escrow. A careful reading of a sample deed of trust form will explain the basics of its use. (See Exhibit 9-5.)

ABSTRACT OF TITLE

An abstract is a history of a piece of land. It begins with a description of the land, then continues as a history of the basics of each and every transaction of this land. These transactions are recorded in chronological sequence.

This history can be used to determine who is the present owner of the land and if the title is clear and unencumbered. To use the abstract as your guide to buying a certain tract of land, you should do the following.

1. Obtain from the seller the abstract to the land.
2. Be sure that the abstract has a signed certificate from a reliable abstracter.
3. Have your real estate lawyer examine the abstract and render his opinion as to the condition of the title.
4. Consider if you wish to obtain title insurance as further protection.

CERTIFICATE OF TITLE

In some areas an abstract is not necessary. An attorney examines the public records and then issues a certificate of title. In areas of its use, it is considered sufficient evidence of good title.

SALE CONTRACTS

It has been said that the contract for sale of real estate is more important than the deed. The reason for this importance is that a properly written sales contract contains all the information that will appear in the deed, plus the method of payment and the delivery date. You are, in fact, dealing with the basic instrument of the real estate business.

FORM NO. 6—CLASS E   DEMAREE STATIONERY CO., 908 Walnut, Kansas City, Mo.

This Deed.   Made and entered into this   day of
One Thousand Nine Hundred and   by and between

part   of the first part, and
party of the second part, and
of   , part   of the third part,
WITNESSETH: That the part   of the first part, in consideration of the debt and trust hereinafter
mentioned and created, and of the sum of One Dollar to   paid by the said part
of the second part, the receipt of which is hereby acknowledged, do by these presents grant, bargain, and
sell, convey and confirm unto the said part   of the second part the following described Real Estate
situate in the County of   in the State of Missouri:

and possession of said premises now delivered unto said part   of the second part.
TO HAVE AND TO HOLD THE SAME, with the appurtenances, to the said part   of the second part, and to his successors hereinafter designated, and to the assigns of him and his successors forever:
IN TRUST, HOWEVER, For the following purposes: WHEREAS, the said

did on the   day of   19   , make and deliver to

NOW THEREFORE, If the said part   of the first part, or anyone for   shall well and truly pay off
and discharge the debt and interest expressed in the said Note   and every part thereof, when the same becomes due
and payable, according to the true tenor, date and effect of said note   , Then This Deed shall be void, and the property hereinbefore conveyed shall be released at the cost of the said part   of the first part; but should the said first
part   fail or refuse to pay the said debt or the said interest or any part thereof, when the same or any part thereof
shall become due and payable, according to the true tenor, date and effect of said Note   , then the whole shall become
due and payable and this deed shall remain in force, and the said part   of the second part or in case of
absence, death or refusal to act, or disability in any wise, when any advertisement and sale are to be made hereunder, then, whoever
shall be sheriff of   County, Missouri, at the time when any such advertisement
and sale are to be made (who shall thereupon for the purpose of that advertisement and sale succeed to the second party's
title to said real estate and the trust herein created respecting the same), may proceed to sell the property hereinbefore
described or any part thereof, at public vendue to the highest bidder at the   in

for cash, first giving   days' public notice of the time, terms and place of sale and of the
property to be sold, by advertisement in some newspaper printed and published in the
of   and upon such sale shall execute and deliver a deed in FEE SIMPLE of the
property sold to the purchaser or purchasers thereof, and receive the proceeds of said sale, and any statement of facts or
recital by the said Trustee, in relation to the non-payment of the money secured to be paid, the advertisement, sale, receipt
of the money and the execution of the deed to the purchaser shall be received as prima facie evidence of such fact; and
such Trustee shall out of the proceeds of such sale pay first, the costs and expenses of executing this trust, including legal
compensation to the Trustee for   services; and next,   shall apply the proceeds remaining
over to the payment of said debt and interest, or so much thereof as remains unpaid, and the remainder, if any, shall be
paid to the said part   of the first part or   legal representatives. And the said part   of the
second part covenant   faithfully to perform and fulfill the trust herein created, not being liable for any mischance
occasioned by others.
IN WITNESS WHEREOF, The said first part   ha   hereunto set   hand   the day and
year first above written.

Signed, sealed and delivered in the presence of us:

_____ _____

_____ _____

_____ _____

_____ _____ .

Courtesy of Demaree Stationery Company, 908 Walnut, Kansas City, Missouri

Exhibit 9-5. Deed of Trust

MISSOURI ACKNOWLEDGMENT—MAN AND WIFE

STATE OF_____

County of_____ } ss.   On this_____day of_____, 19____

before me,_____, a Notary Public, personally appeared

_____and_____

his wife, to me known to be the persons described in and who executed the foregoing instrument, and acknowledged that they executed the same as their free act and deed.

IN TESTIMONY WHEREOF, I have hereunto set my hand and affixed my official seal at

my office in_____the day and year last above written.

My term expires_____, 19____   _____

Notary Public in and for said County and State.

MISSOURI ACKNOWLEDGMENT—UNMARRIED PERSON

STATE OF_____

County of_____ } ss.   On this_____day of_____, 19____

before me,_____, a Notary Public, personally appeared

_____

to me known to be the person described in and who executed the foregoing instrument, and acknowledged that_____

executed the same as_____free act and deed. And the said_____

further declare_____to be single and unmarried.

IN TESTIMONY WHEREOF, I have hereunto set my hand and affixed my official seal at

my office in_____the day and year last above written.

My term expires_____, 19____   _____

Notary Public in and for said County and State.

Deed of Trust

FROM

TO

FOR

Trustees.

Filed for record this_____day

of_____, A.D., 19____

at_____o'clock_____minutes.____M.

Recorded in Book_____at Page_____

Recorder.

By_____Deputy.

Recorder's Fee, $_____

STATE OF_____

County of_____ } ss.   IN THE RECORDER'S OFFICE

I,_____, Recorder of said County, do hereby certify that the within

instrument of writing was, at_____o'clock and_____minutes_____M., on the_____day of_____

A.D., 19____, duly filed for record in my office, and is recorded in the records of this office, in book_____, at page_____

IN WITNESS WHEREOF, I have hereunto set my hand and affixed my official seal at_____

this_____day of_____   _____AD., 19____

_____Recorder.

Courtesy of Demaree Stationery Company, 908 Walnut, Kansas City, Missouri

Exhibit 9-5. Deed of Trust (Continued)

Sales contracts have many names and range from a few sentences to many pages. In general, because it is a contract, it must contain those certain basics of a contract. It must define the intent of both parties in an understandable manner. It must be definite in detail and time. (See Exhibit 9-6.)

CONDITIONAL OR CONTINGENT CONTRACTS

It is common practice to have sales agreements that are subject to certain conditions. Such a conditional or contingent contract must be carefully prepared. It must clearly state what the conditions or contingencies are and how they are to be fulfilled.

If, for example, the condition is based on the sale of another piece of property, then this other property must be described and the acceptable price noted and further defined as to conditions of sale. Another example is in obtaining a loan to pay for the property being purchased. Here we must be definite—the agreement must state the minimum amount of the loan, the maximum interest, and the minimum time for repayment. A loan requirement without definite details would leave wide areas of interpretation and dispute.

SIGNATURES, CONSIDERATION AND ESCROW

The properly drawn sales contract should provide for the signature of both parties. Care should be exercised in dealing with an agent of the seller—the signature of such an agent may or may not be binding. Be sure the agent has the right to sign a sales contract and that he has that right attested to in writing.

Normally a consideration should be involved in a sales contract. It is standard practice for the buyer to make a reasonably substantial payment at the signing of a sales contract. The exception to this is in the use of the sales contract form known as the land contract or contract for deed.

It is also general practice for the agent or a third party to hold the monetary consideration and documents pertaining to the sale. This is referred to as escrow. Here both parties are protected during the period of determining if both parties can and do fulfill their part of the conditions of the sales contract.

FORM NO. 254—CLASS E .   DEMAREE STATIONERY CO., 908 Walnut, Kansas City, Mo.

Real Estate Contract

This Contract, *Made and entered into this......................day of...................................19......*
by and between...
.., the seller........, and..
.., the buyer.......,
*WITNESSETH: that seller........ ha........ sold and agree........ to convey as herein provided the following
described real estate, together with all improvements thereon, including heating, lighting and water supply
apparatus and fixtures, linoleum, window shades, venetian blinds, screens, curtain and drapery rods, and awn-
ings, if any, in...County, State of... to-wit:*

*Subject, however, to street, alley and public utilities rights-of-way and building restrictions, driveway easements, party wall
agreements and community contracts, if any, shown of record, for the price and sum of...*
...DOLLARS $................
to be paid by the buyer as follows..DOLLARS $................
at the signing of this contract, the receipt whereof is hereby acknowledged by the seller........and which is deposited with................

as a part of the consideration of the sale; the balance to be paid in the following manner:
...DOLLARS $................
cash on delivery of deed as herein provided, and..

*All deferred payments to be represented by note......., secured by deed of trust or mortgage on above described property containing
usual provisions, drawing interest from date of deed on the terms specified above.*
*The seller........ to pay all taxes, general and special, and all assessments, which are a lien on said property and can be paid at
the date of this contract, except that all general state, county, school and municipal taxes (exclusive of rebates, penalties or interest)
payable during the calendar year in which the deed is delivered, shall be pro-rated between the seller........ and the buyer........ on the
basis of the said calendar year, as of the date of delivery of the deed. If the amount of such taxes cannot then be ascertained, proration shall be computed on the amount of the general taxes for the preceding calendar year...*

*The rental from said property, and the interest on any existing mortgages shall be pro-rated between the seller and the buyer
as of the date of delivery of the deed. The buyer shall reimburse the seller for any deposit held by the mortgagee.*
The seller........ shall, within ten days from the date hereof, deliver to the buyer........ or at the office of.................................
*...a complete abstract of title to said property from the United States
Government to this date with certificates by competent abstractors as to taxes, judgments and mechanics' liens affecting said property.
The buyer........ shall have ten days after such delivery of abstract to examine the same.*
If the title be good, the seller........ shall deliver for the buyer........ at the office of said...
*..Warranty Deed, properly executed and conveying said property
free and clear from all liens and encumbrances whatsoever, except as herein provided; the buyer........ shall then and there pay the
balance, if any, of said cash payment, and deliver to the seller........ the note and deed of trust, if any, hereinbefore provided for, and
furnish the seller........ with insurance policy containing loss clause payable to the seller ...... as.......................interest may appear;
the buyer........ to accept assignment of insurance now in force, paying therefor the unearned value pro-rated at present current rate.*
*If the title is defective the buyer........ shall specify the objections in writing and deliver the same to or for the seller........ at the
office of...within ten days after such delivery of the abstract, the seller........
shall have the defects rectified within thirty days from date of delivery of such objections, but in case such defects in the title cannot
be rectified within that time, this contract shall be null and void, and the money deposited as aforesaid shall be returned to the
buyer........ and the abstract returned to the seller......... Seller........ may, at.......................option, furnish a Title Insurance Policy
on the property herein sold in place of the abstract hereinbefore provided for.*
*If the seller ...... ha....... kept............................part of this contract, by furnishing good title as herein provided, and the
buyer........ fail to comply with the requirements within five days thereafter, then the money deposited as aforesaid shall be forfeited
by the buyer......., and this contract may or may not be thereafter operative, at the option of the seller........*
Time is of the essence of this contract.
IN WITNESS WHEREOF, Said parties hereunto subscribe their names.
Executed in triplicate

....
....
....
....

Courtesy of Demaree Stationery Company, 908 Walnut, Kansas City, Missouri

Exhibit 9-6. Sales Contract

Real Estate Contract

FROM

_____

_____

TO

_____

_____

Price $_____

Property _____

_____

Date _____ 19_____

Abstract ordered _____ 19_____

Abstract delivered _____ 19_____

Attorney's opinion received_____ 19_____

Closed _____ 19_____

Courtesy of Demaree Stationery Company, 908 Walnut, Kansas City, Missouri

Exhibit 9-6. Sales Contract (Continued)

At the time that the parties have met or defaulted on the terms of the sales contract, the third party makes delivery of the documents and monies as prescribed in the sales contract. The third party makes certain that all documents are properly signed and sealed.

CONTRACT ASSIGNMENT

It is legal for a buyer who has a signed sale contract to sell that contract. The buyer actually sells his rights under that contract. In legal terms he assigns, for a consideration, to a person now called the assignee, his rights to purchase the property under the terms of the contract. The assignee can now act with the same authority as the original buyer.

It should be kept in mind that if the assignee does not complete the purchase, the original buyer must do so. The act of assigning the contract does not relieve the original buyer from the terms of the contract. A sales contract can be written in such a manner as to prohibit the assigning of that contract to another party. Such a contract must contain this prohibition in writing.

TRADES, OPTIONS AND ZONING

The three subjects listed above are all covered in detail in other chapters in this book. They are listed here only on the basis of the documents used in relation to each.

TRADES

Normal sales, financing and conveyance of title documents are used in trading. Special attention may be required relative to the dollar amounts shown on the documents used. Tax liabilities may be increased in a trade, the amount of such liability determined by the dollar amounts shown on the documents.

Overpricing of properties in trade deals is very common. This is not bad if both parties are aware that the deal is based on inflated values. If, however, taxes must be paid based on these trade prices, it is foolish to consummate the deal based on such figures.

OPTIONS

An option is a contract or agreement where the owner of property gives to a person or business entity, for a period of time, the right to purchase his property for a specified amount of money, on specified terms and with certain prescribed conditions. There are many differing conditions involved in each option. Because of these varying conditions and requirements, options in general must be written specifically for the specific deal.

ZONING

Again, because this subject is covered in a chapter of its own, it is mentioned here only as it relates to real estate documents. Because zoning affects value, it is important that the buyer be aware if the property in question is zoned, and if zoned, for what use it is zoned.

The zoning should be written into the documents used in the sale and conveyance of zoned property. A sales contract can be written contigent upon the obtaining of a certain type of zoning.

THE GOLDEN CONTRACT

Now you will study what in the opinion of the author is the MOST IMPORTANT DOCUMENT USED IN DEALING IN LAND.

This document has changed the financial fortunes of entire states. This document opened the door to land ownership to millions of middle-and low-income Americans.

This same document is, for the dealer in land, the key to unlimited sales and the profits that result from those sales. If I could put the name of this document in letters ten feet high, I would do just that. The author of this book, based on thousands of sales using this document, does believe that both for the buyer and the seller this is the GOLDEN CONTRACT. Its name is . . .

CONTRACT FOR DEED
also known as the
LAND CONTRACT

A contract for deed or land contract is a method to sell or buy land on an installment basis. It is an installment purchase contractual agreement.

CONTRACT FOR DEED DEFINED

We are dealing with a contract. A contract requires certain elements to be included. As different sales may have special requirements, all contracts for deed are not the same. We will list the elements that should appear in a valid contract for deed. These elements are listed in numerical order as they would normally appear. (See Exhibit 9-7.)

1. Date
2. Name and address of both parties
3. Agreement to sell and agreement to buy
4. Description of property
5. Easements, special rights, zoning and restriction information
6. Special assessments
7. *Purchase price, time charges, payment plan including acknowledgement of down payment
8. Terms under which default may occur. Result of default, including liquidation damages
9. Binding on heirs, executors, administrators and assigns
10. Taxes—who pays
11. Time is the essence
12. Signatures of both parties

THE REASON IT IS GOLDEN

The greatest benefit derived from the use of the contract for deed is that the purchaser can buy property without having any appreciable amount of cash. An example: the author has sold hundreds of thousands of dollars worth of land to thousands of buyers with the down payment being only ONE DOLLAR. Yes, you read that correctly—one dollar down payment. Using the contract for deed as the installment sales instrument, this token

---

*See Special Note on truth in lending law at the end of this chapter.

FORM NO 6B—CLASS E   DEMAREE STATIONERY CO., 908 Walnut, Kansas City. Mo.

Contract for Deed

*THIS AGREEMENT, Between*_____

*party of the first part, hereinafter called the seller, whether one or more, and*_____

_____

part____ of the second part, hereinafter called the buyer, whether one or more.

WITNESSETH: That for the consideration hereinafter specified, the seller hereby sells, and agrees

*to convey to said buyer, the following described land, situated in the County of*_____

*State of*_____, *to-wit:*

*IN CONSIDERATION WHEREOF, Said buyer hereby promises to pay the seller*_____

_____*Dollars, as follows:*

_____*Dollars in hand, and*

_____*Dollars*

*on the*_____*day of*_____, *19____, and*

_____*Dollars*

*on or before the*_____*day of each succeeding month thereafter with interest at*_____*per*

*cent per annum, interest payable*_____*until the*

*amount of*_____*Dollars has been paid.*

and to pay all taxes and special assessments hereafter becoming due and payable against said land and all improvements
*made thereon.*_____
If said buyer fails to pay any such taxes or special assessments before penalty or interest accrues thereon, or when
the same may or should be paid, or if said land or any part thereof be sold for non-payment of taxes or special assess-
ments, then the seller may pay such delinquent taxes or special assessments, or redeem the property from any tax
sale, in which case the buyer shall repay the amount or amounts so expended, with interest on all so expended from
dates of expenditure at the rate of eight per cent per annum until paid. The buyer to have possession of said real estate
from this time.

On full payment of the sums of money and interest aforesaid, including all expended by the seller on account of
taxes and special assessments and redemption from tax sales, the seller shall convey said land to the said buyer by
deed duly acknowledged or proved, containing a covenant that the seller is well seized of said land at the date hereof,
and a covenant against encumbrances, and warranting title as of date hereof.

*And the said buyer shall and will at*_____*own expense from the date of the execution of this Contract*
until said payments and interest, and all liens and charges by virtue hereof, are fully paid off and discharged, keep the
building—erected, and to be erected on said lands, in some responsible insurance company duly authorized to
*do business in the State of*_____*to the amount*

_____*Dollars,*
for the benefit of the seller or his assigns; and in default thereof seller may, at his option, effect such insurance in his
own name, and the premium or premiums, cost, charges and expenses for effecting the same shall be an additional lien
on said property, and may, at his option, pay any taxes or statutory liens against said property, all of which sums with
_____*per cent interest may be enforced and collected in the same manner as the principal debt hereby secured.*

It is expressly understood and agreed that Time Is the Essence of This Contract and that if the buyer shall fail to
*pay any installment, interest, taxes, lien or other payment for a period of*_____*days after said payment*
shall become due and payable, then the amount theretofore paid by the buyer shall, at the option of the seller, be for-
feited to the seller as liquidated damages for breach of this contract, and on such default, it will be lawful and proper
for the seller, or its assigns, without notice, to take possession of said premises, and it is further agreed that upon
such default the buyer shall then become a tenant of the seller as a tenant from month to month and agrees to pay
_____*Dollars per month as rent for such premises, said rent becoming due and*
payable monthly in advance.

It is mutually agreed that all covenants and agreements herein contained shall extend to and be obligatory upon the
heirs, executors, administrators, successors and assigns of the respective parties.

*IN WITNESS WHEREOF, The said parties have hereunto set their hands and seal this*_____

*day of*_____*A. D., 19____*

EXECUTED IN DUPLICATE   _____

_____

Courtesy of Demaree Stationery Company, 908 Walnut, Kansas City, Missouri

Exhibit 9-7. Contract for Deed

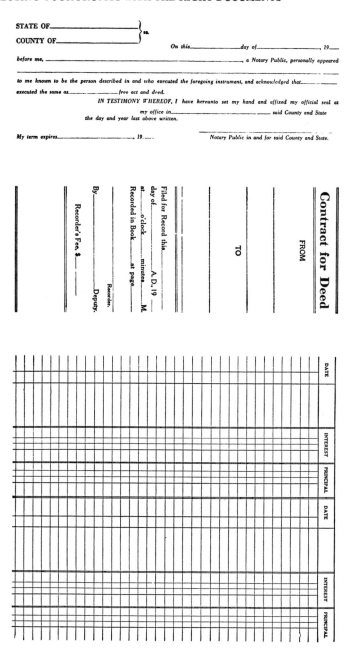

STATE OF_____ } ss.
COUNTY OF_____ }

On this_____day of_____, 19___

before me, _____, a Notary Public, personally appeared

_____

to me known to be the person described in and who executed the foregoing instrument, and acknowledged that_____
executed the same as_____free act and deed.
          IN TESTIMONY WHEREOF, I have hereunto set my hand and affixed my official seal at
                    my office in_____ said County and State
          the day and year last above written.

My term expires_____, 19____.   _____
                                                        Notary Public in and for said County and State.

Courtesy of Demaree Stationery Company, 908 Walnut, Kansas City, Missouri

Exhibit 9-7. Contract for Deed (Continued)

down payment method has been profitable for the seller, and it has resulted in thousands of happy, satisfied land owners.

The reason you can profitably sell low priced lots for one dollar down using the contract for deed is based on the advantage of the Golden Contract. Here are the main points of this advantage.

CONTRACT FOR DEED

1. Buyer obtains possession without title.
2. Seller need not have clear title to the land at time of sale.
3. No outside financing is needed.
4. Repossession in case of buyer default is easy, quick and inexpensive.
5. The credit standing of the buyer is of much less importance.

Let us now examine each of these five points individually.

Point One

Buyer obtains possession without title. At the signing of the contract for deed, the buyer is allowed to take possession of the property described in the contract. This possession is based on his continued performance of the terms of the contract. The buyer must complete the terms of the contract before he receives title to the described property.

Point Two

Seller need not have clear title to the land he sells.

It is not necessary for the seller to have unencumbered property in order to sell that property using the contract for deed. As the title will not be conveyed until a later date, the seller must only have the ability to deliver an unencumbered title at the date of completion of the terms of the contract for deed.

An example: You buy 100 acres for $100 per acre—total price $10,000. You buy this land using a contract for deed. You pay $500 down and will pay the balance on monthly payments. You also have a release clause in the contract. This clause allows you to obtain title to any acre tract of this property upon your paying a specified amount of money. For the sake of this example, we will say that you can obtain title to any specified acre of this land upon payment of $250.

You now sell acre tracts of this land for $695 each. You sell these tracts on terms, using the contract for deed. You take $25 down and $25 per month. You do not have unencumbered title to the land you have sold. You do have the legal contract that makes it possible for you to obtain title at any time you need such title.

You are in an entirely legal position. You have, by using the Golden Contract, been able to engage in a fairly large-scale land deal with a very limited investment. Then, by selling lots or tracts using the same type contract, you can actually use your customers' money to pay for your purchase and give you a substantial profit.

GOLDEN MONEY LEVERAGE

Let us now do the mathematics of this example. We can see the dollars and cents side of the use of the Golden Contract for Deed.

1.	Total price of land	$10,000
2.	You paid $500 Down	500
3.	You financed by contract for deed	9,500
4.	Interest cost for terms, est.	2,000
5.	Total time cost of land (including down payment)	$12,000
6.	You sell 100 one acre tracts for $695 ea.	69,500
7.	You received one hundred $25 down payments	$ 2,500
8.	You receive 36 monthly payments of $25 for ea. of the 100 lots	
	Total	$90,000
9.	You actually receive, including interest, a total gross income of	$90,000
10.	Estimating advertising and sales costs at 25%, plus survey, roads, etc.	$47,000
11.	You have made a profit of	$43,000

This was accomplished with a down payment of only $500, a small amount of operating capital, and the Golden Contract.

Reread this example—examine the facts, figures, and profits. You will be able to see why the contract for deed is indeed Golden.

Point Three

No outside financing is needed.

The contract for deed is the agreement most commonly used by the seller when he is financing the sale himself. The elements that you are now considering make this contract the best way to eliminate the need for a third party as the source of financing. In most cases this results in less cost for the buyer and added profits for the seller.

Point Four

Repossession in case of buyer default is easy, quick, and inexpensive.

In a properly written contract for deed, the time from buyer default to seller being able to resell is at most 90 days. The costs involved can be as little as a certified letter advising of the default. This results in none of the problems that accrue from issuing title and taking back a mortgage.

Point Five

The credit standing of the buyer is of much less importance. This is because the buyer does not receive title to the property until he has completed the payments under the terms of the contract. The seller delivers only possession, not title. In fact, the seller has given nothing except use, and that use only as long as the buyer is in compliance with the terms of the contract.

The buyer must perform as he agrees or he not only does not receive title to the property, but he loses any monies he has paid on the property. The seller merely gives legal notice of the default, and when the time period has passed, the seller can resell the property.

UNDERSTAND HOW TO USE

Read the sample Land Contract Agreement. (See Exhibit 9-8.) Study it to be sure you really understand each element in the contract. Check the time charge and the time element. If in doubt, ask your real estate lawyer to go over such contracts point by point.

To really understand the many uses of the contract for deed is to know the basis of your spare time fortune in land.

BELIEVE

If this sounds too good to be true, believe it any way—use the contract for deed on a small project. Test it; prove it. Once you have enjoyed the profits from the use of the contract for deed, you will join the author in calling it the Golden Contract.

THE MORTGAGE

The mortgage is a conveyance of real property on a conditional basis, such conveyance to be used as security for an obligation. The mortgage must contain the names of the borrower and the lender, the details of the loan involved, what part of the property is obligated, a description of the property, and the mortgage covenants. The mortgage must be signed, acknowledged, and delivered.

There are many sub-forms of mortgages. The most common is the second or junior mortgage, which is a mortgage that is subordinate to another mortgage. Other types of mortgages are blanket mortgages, open end mortgages, construction loan mortgages, and many more.

You do not pay on a mortgage. You pay on the obligation that the mortgage secures. This obligation is generally in the form of a note. Special information: In certain areas of our country, the mortgage is not considered a conveyance. In these areas the mortgage is, in effect, a lien on the property until the obligation is paid. Here again, use a competent lawyer to be certain you follow the correct legal procedure.

STATE OF MISSOURI   )   KIRK C. COLONY, INC.
) SS.
COUNTY OF _____)   CONTRACT FOR DEED

     THIS AGREEMENT, made and entered into this _____ day of _____,
19_____, by and between KIRK C. COLONY, INC., hereinafter referred to as "SELLER,"
and _____ of the county of _____,
State of _____, hereinafter referred to as "BUYER."

     WITNESSETH: That on the terms and conditions herein contained, the SELLER
agrees to sell and convey by Warranty Deed to the BUYER, Tract or Lot No. _____
_____, _____ subdivision, plat of said
subdivision appearing on record in the Recorder of Deeds Office, _____
County, Missouri.

     1. The BUYER agrees to purchase said property and pay therefor the Cash Price
of _____ Dollars ($_____),
payable by the BUYER either in full upon the execution of this contract or as follows:

     2. TOTAL CASH DOWN PAYMENT _____
_____ Dollars ($_____).

     3. UNPAID BALANCE of cash price and amount financed (line 1 less line 2)
_____ Dollars ($_____).

     4. The AMOUNT FINANCED shall be paid in _____ monthly installments of
_____Dollars ($_____), the first
installment being payable _____, 19_____, and all subsequent
installments on the same day of each consecutive month until paid in full.,
TOTAL OF PAYMENTS_____ Dollars ($_____).

     5. FINANCE CHARGE (line 2 plus line 4 less line 1) _____
_____ Dollars ($_____).

     6. DEFERRED PAYMENT PRICE (line 1 plus line 5) _____
_____ Dollars ($_____).

     The unpaid balance of the cash price (amount financed) recited herein bears
_____ per cent (_____%) ANNUAL PERCENTAGE RATE interest.

     All payments under this contract shall be made to the _____
_____.
When the purchase price is fully paid, the SELLER shall execute and deliver, or cause
to be delivered, to the BUYER, a Warranty Deed conveying said property to the BUYER.
Said warranty deed shall be subject to easements., restrictions and covenants of record.

Courtesy of Kirk C. Colony of Ozarks, Inc., Kansas City, Missouri

Exhibit 9-8. Land Contract Agreement

But in all cases, time is the essence of this contract; and if default of 60 days is made in any installment when due, the SELLER shall have the right to rescind this agreement; and all monies paid hereunder and all buildings and construction of any kind on said property shall be retained by the SELLER as agreed liquidated damages and rent of said property.

A letter addressed to the BUYER at _____
_____ shall be sufficient notice of the exercise of such option by the SELLER.

THE BUYER and SELLER agree that all taxes on the property covered by this contract shall be prorated as of the date of this contract. The BUYER shall pay all subsequent taxes against said property, promptly as they accrue.

The restrictions upon all lot owners attached hereto and by this reference made a part hereof shall be considered a part of this contract.

No assignment or transfer of this contract by the BUYER shall be binding on the SELLER unless an assignment is endorsed upon this contract and the name and address of the assignee is furnished by the BUYER to the SELLER and the assignee signs a written assumption of this contract and agrees to its terms.

This contract is not binding upon the SELLER until executed by one of its duly authorized officers or agents. It is understood and agreed that there are no terms or conditions to this sale other than those appearing in this contract. Executed in _____ upon the day and date first above written.

I have read the above contract
and attached restrictions.

```
            (
            (
BUYER:      ( _____
            (
            (
            ( _____
```

KIRK C. COLONY, INC.

By_____

Exhibit 9-8. Land Contract Agreement (Continued)

TITLE INSURANCE

Title insurance is a policy defending the holder against loss due to title defects. The use of title insurance in buying and selling real estate can be of great assistance in obtaining required financing. Some lending agencies will not consider making a real estate loan unless the borrower can furnish a title insurance policy. Title insurance companies and their representatives are located in all major cities and county seat towns.

For a fee, a title insurance company will do a title search and issue a title policy based on the results of such search. The policy issued will insure those named against loss and damage up to the amount of the insurance.

A SUGGESTION

In dealing with the title to land, it is the author's suggestion that the buyer visit the local abstract company. Here are people conversant with the local land, its history, and its present owners. Much valuable help and information is available from such firms.

REAL ESTATE FORMS AS SALES AIDS

The successful dealer in land must always be selling his product. Most professional real estate people tend to overlook the sales value inherent in the forms and documents used in the sale of real property. This, I believe, is the result of familiarity breeding not only contempt but the ability to look but not see.

The prospective land buyer is engaged in a major decision. He is suffering from doubt and anxiety. He can change his mind for reasons that the seller cannot understand. The job of the seller is to reassure the prospect. The wording of the documents used in consummating the sale can be used for that purpose.

THE SELLING SALES CONTRACT

If the seller has prepared his sales contract properly, it will help create a feeling of legal security. Now if the buyer is shown the parts of the contract that protect him, if the special words are explained, if the buyer knows what the warranty of the warranty deed really means, the ordinary contract of sale properly used becomes a sales aid. (See Exhibit 9-8.)

Some land dealers have a purchase certificate that is so attractive that many buyers have it framed. The buyer is proud to be a landowner. This pride can be used to sell more land to the original owner's friends and relatives. Give the buyer something to tell other people. Help him have that extra knowledge about the papers he is expected to sign. He will have less of those feelings of doubt. He will also feel that he can explain his good deal to his associates. From this happy, knowledgeable buyer will come more sales for you.

Each form you use to sell land should be legal, and should look legal. Have these forms prepared right. Don't frighten the prospect with rough, dirty, dog-eared forms. Ask yourself, would you want to sign such forms? You, the seller, must be able to answer the buyer's questions regarding all the words and meanings contained in the forms.

You have the responsibility to know your product and your business. You are the dealer in land. Your prospects must be convinced of your knowledge and integrity. You will be successful only if you make sure you are helping the buyer to make his decisions. He needs information and assistance to arrive at this decision to spend his money to purchase your land. Be sure you are competent to fill his need.

The appearance of your documents, their ability to stand examination by the buyer's lawyer, plus your ability to explain their meaning is as important in selling land as the product or your advertising. The documents used in dealing in land are not only necessary to complete the sale, they are the tools that can make the dealer in land his fortune.

SPECIAL NOTE

Time charges are subject to the truth in lending laws. Be certain that all sales contracts and sales agreements comply with this law. It is also possible that the Right of Rescission may apply; again, check with your lawyer or contact the appropriate governmental agencies.

10

The "Sell Some--Hold Some" Fortune-Building Technique

Now you will learn a method of dealing in land that is probably as old as the history of land transactions. No doubt the earliest records of buying and selling of land would record where this procedure was used for profit. Here you can learn the Sell Some–Hold Some method of dealing in land. We will define, explain, and by example show how you can use the Sell Some–Hold Some method to gain profit and financial security.

DEFINITION

The Sell Some–Hold Some method of dealing land can be defined as follows. You buy a tract of land; you sell part of that tract for as much or more than you paid for the entire tract, and you hold the remaining part of the tract for future appreciation and profit.

You can readily understand from the definition that the Sell Some–Hold Some method, if used and re-used, could only result in profits and an increase in assets.

THE BASICS OF THE METHOD

1. You buy the right land at the right price.
2. You sell a portion of this land at a price higher than the total cost of all the land.

3. You hold the balance of this land as part of your estate until you decide to sell.

THE PROFIT PAYS FOR YOUR LAND

This is, in essence, the wonderful Sell Some—Hold Some method of dealing in land. You're buying land, selling part of it at a profit, and using part or all of this profit to pay for all of the land. This leaves you with land that you own free and clear.

Here you own land with no investment except your time. The value of your estate has grown and will grow even more. You have been tax sheltered, you have used the sell some, hold some method to establish the base for your financial security, and, if you desire, for profits today.

AN EXAMPLE OF THE METHOD IN ACTION

You purchase a piece of land costing $1,500 but your only cash outlay at this time will be no more than $500 as your down payment. You can easily finance the balance of $1,000 with the owner, using a contract as follows. The contract between you and the seller would be on this basis, the land to be divided into ten tracts. (See Exhibit 10-1.) Each tract to be valued at $150. Your down payment of $500 releases four of these tracts. This means that you can resell four tracts at any time without further payment. The contract further agrees that you may make additional payments of $150 at any time. Each time you make such a payment you are to receive title to one tract. A time period in which you must complete the total purchase of all tracts is incorporated in the agreement.

You now have control over the entire property. You have an initial cash outlay of only $500, and you have the right to sell four of the tracts. Putting into effect any of a number of the selling methods outlined in this book, you can now sell all four of these tracts at a profit. Then, using your profits, you can pay off the balance due on the entire property.

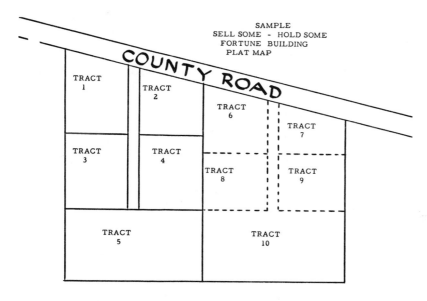

NOTE: TRACTS 1-2-3-4-5 ARE SURVEYED AND THE ROAD
TO THE TRACT IS ACTUALLY BUILT.

TRACTS 6-7-8-9-10 ARE NOT SURVEYED AND THE ROAD
TO THESE TRACTS IS NOT BUILT. THIS LEAVES APPROXIMATELY
ONE HALF OF THE PROPERTY TO BE USED ACCORDING TO THIS
PLAT OR CHANGED TO SUIT FUTURE NEEDS OR DESIRES.

Courtesy of Kirk C. Colony of Ozarks, Inc., Kansas City, Missouri

Exhibit 10-1. Sample "Sell Some-Hold Some" Fortune Building Plat Map

RESULTS OF USING THE METHOD

Your completion of this land project should be something like
this:

Land cost $1,500
Interest on contract 180
Cost of advertising, survey & road 400

Total Costs $2,080

Your selling price for each tract is $695; you sell five tracts,
resulting in a gross income of $3,475 plus any interest you may

receive for any sales made on time payments. With a total cost for all land, interest, advertising, survey and road of $2,080 and a gross income from five tracts of $3,475, you have made a profit of $1,395 and you have a clear title to one half of the original land. Following this procedure, you have used the Sell Some—Hold Some method to acquire land at no cost, and in addition, you have made a substantial immediate profit.

INCREASE YOUR ASSETS

You will note that we did not execute a survey of the entire ten tracts. We did not build a road in the unsold area. This leaves you with complete flexibility in the future development of this property. By not doing these things at this point in time, we also reduced the initial cash needed.

You have just followed a series of actions that are available to any dealer in land. You have seen how you can make an actual cash profit and how you now own land that has cost you nothing but your effort. You have been able to increase your earnings and at the same time increase your assets.

GAIN FINANCIAL SECURITY

You now have the key to a future made more secure, a future that can be filled with both personal satisfaction and financial security. Visualize five, ten, twenty years from now. You have continued to develop your land ventures. How many acres of land might you own? The author of this book, applying the Sell Some—Hold Some system, can only estimate the total acres he now owns. He does know that this land can and will take care of him financially for the rest of his life.

The use of this system is not only the key, it is the doorway to financial security.

ISLAND PROFITS

An actual example: The author of this book purchases 67 acres of land on Padre Island on the Gulf of Mexico for $20,000. This land was then subdivided into 117 lots, plus a marina site and a motel site. In the first two years of ownership 41 lots were sold, for a total gross income of approximately $36,000. The author today holds clear title to 76 lots plus the marina site and the motel site. The value of this area has increased many times since the date of the original purchase. We see the Sell Some–Hold Some method allowed the author to pay for the entire tract, make a profit, and still own over 50 percent of the tract, including the most valuable areas. The author is holding the balance of this land for the time when certain factors create the best selling climate. It costs less than $400 per year in taxes, and because it is land without improvements, there is no maintenance or upkeep.

BUY, SELL, HOLD AND PROSPER

Buy a tract, sell some lots, hold the remainder for time and change to increase the value and salability. This is the basis of the Sell Some–Hold Some method. The basis of your fortune in land may well be the use and reuse of this method. Project in your mind your ownership of tracts of land in various places, paid for by others, owned by you. Here can be your annuity at the cost of only your effort. Here is a system that can be tailored to your desires. Here is a system that can be tested in some cases with no risk of your capital. It is not impossible to buy land without a down payment if the seller sees that he can participate in the profits from your labors. He may well join you and put up his land as his part of the deal.

DEALING IN LAND WITH NO CASH

Example: A owns 100 acres near the city. He may have inherited this land; in any event, it is just sitting there. A has either no cost in the land or a very low per-acre cost. You are B—you say to A, "I believe I can make this land profitable. I will sign a contract to purchase your land at so much an acre plus a percent of the gross price I receive when I resell any part of the property." A retains title to the property until he receives payment for any portion you sell or until you pay him the agreed per-acre price. You pay an agreed minimum amount per each lot or tract as it is sold, plus the agreed percentage. A is assured that any land he actually deeds gives him an adequate return. You make the difference as a profit for your efforts, and using this profit to pay off the unsold portion, you can in time own a substantial part of the land with only the percentage, generally 10 to 15 percent, to be paid when you sell the remaining land. This is one of the several ways you can deal in land without any cash investment in the land itself.

FINANCIAL SECURITY USING THE METHOD

Now a recap of the Sell Some–Hold Some method of dealing in land. Why use this method? The answer is that it allows you to acquire paid-for land without having your capital tied up for a long period. This is possible because you sell part at a profit and use the profit to pay for the balance. You can, by repeating this procedure, become a major land owner and never allow yourself to be in debt for more than one piece of property at a time. With the passage of years, you will reach the point where you will have varied landholdings all free and clear. Once you have accomplished this, you are as nearly secure financially as anyone can be in this world. That is the why of the Sell Some–Hold Some method.

HOW TO DO IT

Now as to the HOW—reread this entire chapter, then act; start becoming an expert on a certain area or type of land. This can be a pleasure—weekend drives with a meaning. The learning process can be enjoyable when it gets you out in the fresh air; out among people. Ask questions, stop in a filling station, cafes—talk to the local officials; be pleasant, be friendly; and you will, in most cases, be treated courteously, and you will get valuable information. Do not be bothered by the fact that the local people can remember when land in the area was selling for $2.00-$10.00 an acre You already know that the force that makes that $2.00-per-acre ground sell for $100 per acre now will be working for you in the future. It always seems that it takes an outsider to recognize the local opportunities.

PROFIT FROM 1500 MILES AWAY

I know of a valuable piece of land at the entrance to a new major airport. It was sold to the airport by a man who lives over 1,500 miles from the airport. How did this man become the owner of this valuable property? Believe it or not, he was a salesman for a company that was selling to an airline that was located in the area that was just being talked about as the airport site. This salesman heard the employees of the airline talk about the fact that some day there might be an airport in this area. The salesman bought a large parcel of land on the basis of this information. Eight years later, he sold this land for as many thousands of dollars per acre as he had paid hundreds of dollars per acre. His profit was 1,000 percent and he was taxed at the capital gain's rate. This salesman became a wealthy man from this one transaction. Why didn't the people who told him about this situation buy this land? They would say first they didn't have the money. The salesman used credit to make the purchase—he didn't have the money either. He was willing to use a percentage of his income to make payments on the land to put himself in a position to make a profit. The non-buyers will also say, how could you be sure that the airport would become a reality? The answer—you couldn't be sure. Let's assume that the airport plan had been dropped. Farm land prices in areas near, but not involved in the airport, have doubled and tripled in value in the eight-year period involved. We see that our salesman friend would have made a very profitable investment without the airport. He was also able to rent this land for grazing and had an income. He could also have used our Sell Some–Hold Some method, and been in a no loss, all profit position no matter what happened.

ARE YOU A DOER?

The non-buyers really just didn't have the foresight and the courage to buy the land. Very few people will admit that those are the real reasons they don't do things. It is much easier to say some people are lucky. You can start being lucky just as soon as you decide to be a doer instead of a watcher.

Our point is, the local people may not appreciate the acres of money right under their noses. Get advice, get facts, study them carefully, then make your own decision. You must be a self-starter to succeed as a dealer in land. Even a mistake can be rectified and turned into a profit. The author's first major real estate venture seemed doomed to failure.

LOCAL ADVICE CAN BACKFIRE

I took the local real estate man's advice: I made the first lots too large; I put the road in the wrong place, and I couldn't sell one lot for a price I could make a profit from. It wasn't long before I decided that spending my weekends watching prospects come and go without a sale was not going to make my fortune. I started asking questions of the prospective buyers. Their answers soon told me that I needed smaller lots, needed to sell on terms, and that they would not buy a lot where the road was so steep as to make the women nervous. I had planned my first subdivision without testing what the public wanted. I have not made that mistake again.

CHANGE MADE THE DIFFERENCE

To finish this incident, I changed location within the same piece of property. I subdivided into smaller lots, was more careful about my roads so they did not have any steep hills, and then with smaller lots, I reduced my price per lot yet still retained my desired profit margin. I offered terms, and I sold over fifty lots in two weeks.

YOU ARE NOT THE BUYER

You must accept the fact that you are not going to buy your own property; what you would buy is different from that which you are selling. You are the wholesale buyer—you are the retail seller. You buy large—you sell small. Do not confuse what would appeal to you with that which will appeal to the masses. You have already demonstrated that you are not the average person; reading a book such as this removes you from the average buyer of a lot or small tract of land. I want to be sure you do not make the mistake of trying to sell based on what you would buy. Find out what the average man is looking for—that is the key to sales.

YOU CREATE THE ACTION

Remember, you are using the Sell Some–Hold Some method; this means you are selling part of your property in the same year that you have purchased it. This does not allow time to help add value. You must make the changes that add the value. You must offer the land in such a manner that people will pay you more than you paid. In the sell some, hold some method, you create the action.

TAX SHELTER

We must all devote a portion of our financial planning to the subject of income taxes. The Sell Some–Hold Some method does offer certain tax advantages. Using this method, you can actually increase your assets without any tax liability being incurred. The following example will give you the details of how this can be accomplished. The figures used are fictitious, but the details are actual.

PURCHASE, SELL, HOLD, PROFIT

You purchase ten acres of land; your original land cost is $400 per acre. Your total land cost for all ten acres is $4,000. You subdivide five acres of this land into twenty lots. Your cost for surveying, road building, etc., is $750. You then sell these twenty lots for $350 each. This brings you a total gross income of $7,000. You spent $250 for advertising and miscellaneous expense pertaining to the sale of these lots. You now have a project that is basically as follows.

COSTS

Original ten acres at $400 per acre
Total land cost $4,000
Deductible expenditures on five acres
    (This is cost of survey, roads, advertising & misc.) $1,000
                                           $5,000

TAX COMPUTATION

In computing your tax cost base for the twenty lots, you can only use the land cost of five acres. This is because you have only used five acres to obtain the twenty lots.

Land cost for twenty lots (five acres) $2,000
Cost for survey, roads, advertising, miscellaneous $1,000
Total tax deductible cost basis $3,000
With your selling price of $350 per lot,
    your gross income is $7,000
Your deductible cost is $3,000
Your taxable income is $4,000
Based on 30 percent your tax is $1,200
This leaves you an after-tax profit of $2,800

NOW YOU OWN PAID-FOR LAND

You use $2,000 of the after-tax profit to pay for the remaining unimproved five acres of land. The result of this deal is that you now own five acres of land valued at not less than $2,000. You own this land free and clear. All income taxes are paid, and you also have a profit in cash of $800.

TIME SALES CAN ADD PROFITS

If the sale of the twenty lots had been on terms spread over three or four years, the tax liability would have been substantially reduced. You would also have made additional profit from the interest you charged.

YOU CAN CONVERT TO CASH

You now have an asset in the five acres you retained. This asset can be used as collateral to raise tax-free cash. By borrowing money on this five acres you will have money that you can use to make more land investments. Here you can make additional investments without using any money from your regular income.

ASSETS FROM PROFITS

The Sell Some—Hold Some method makes it possible for the land dealer to continuously add to his assets. He can do this with the least tax liability, and even this is paid for from the profits received from the Sell Some part. The Hold Some part is completely tax sheltered until you sell and profit from the land you are holding.

THE PYRAMID TO WEALTH

You have learned the basics of the Sell Some—Hold Some method of dealing in land. Now, you will learn how easy it can be to use your experience, profits, and increased net worth to pyramid to the really big money. Cash plus credit are the ingredients that make pyramiding possible.

ONE DEAL LEADS TO ANOTHER

Your first Sell Some—Hold Some deal has given you a small amount of cash, plus a larger credit base. You now have an asset that can be used as collateral for a bank loan. Using the cash on hand from the profit on your first deal plus the cash you receive from the loan on the land you are holding, you are now ready for your second Sell Some—Hold Some land deal.

YOUR EXPERIENCE PAYS

You are not an amateur on your second land deal. You have experience and the start of a reputation. One successful deal leads to another as the word spreads that you are an action person. You begin to recognize that all the world respects the person who does things. As you negotiate your second land deal, the seller, the lender, and even the prospective customers will show you more respect. More importantly, they will be more cooperative. You have proven you are a person worth dealing with. You now will have stature. You are now profiting from both your experience and your reputation.

THE SECOND DEAL AND HOW IT WORKS

You now purchase land, using the cash you received from the Sell Some part of deal number one. Added to this cash is the cash you get from a loan on the land you own from the Hold Some part of your first deal. Now, repeating the method used in your Sell Some–Hold Some deal number one, the results will be identical in detail, and for purposes of example we will assume the amounts of money will also be the same. This results in your financial situation at the conclusion of your second deal as follows.

DOUBLE YOUR PROFIT, DOUBLE YOUR ASSETS

1. Your original cash has been returned
2. You have repaid the loan on deal number one land
3. You have made a profit on deal number two
4. You have obtained additional land free and clear from deal number two

Based on deal number two being the same size as deal number one, the results of both deals combined and shown in dollars and assets would be as follows.

1. You now have $1,600 in cash
2. You now own $4,000 worth of land
3. You now have no debts
4. You have made at least $5,600.

You have none of your own money invested, yet you are $5,600 ahead. You have also gained both experience and reputation as a money-making dealer in land.

$20,000 AND $40,000 IS JUST AS EASY

For illustrative purposes, we have used the amounts of $800 and $1,600 to show profits. As you have read in the actual examples of Sell Some–Hold Some deals, this could be $8,000 and $16,000, or even $20,000 and $40,000. It is up to you at what level you start. It is also up to you as to how many times you want to pyramid your profits.

WE ARE DEALING WITH A FORTUNE

The Sell Some–Hold Some method of dealing in land in your spare time is a sound, proven method. The degree of success, the amount of wealth accumulation, is governed mainly by the dealer. Think big, and it is a fact, you may think your way to a fortune.

THE SELL SOME–HOLD SOME METHOD AND YOUR FUTURE

You have now, in this chapter, traveled and retraveled the road of the Sell Some–Hold Some method of dealing in land. To be sure we understand this method, let's repeat the basics one more time. You buy a piece of property, you sell part of it for enough to pay for all of it; now you own a piece of property with no cost to you except your effort. Do this a number of times and you will wake up some morning and realize you are a wealthy person. Read and reread this chapter and do not attempt your first land deal until you have read all of this book. They say a little knowledge is a dangerous thing. Don't become overconfident; proceed carefully; get good legal advice; become knowledgeable; then act—and act decisively.

11

Effective Psychology
That Sells Land

It doesn't seem logical or sensible to say that because the majority of people think small you can make money. It is, however, a provable fact that in dealing in land, this think small syndrome sells millions of dollars worth of lots and small tracts of land. You are dealing with one of the most effective psychological sales methods you will ever learn.

There is a psychological barrier in almost all people's minds. Their brain says stop—don't do it. It says this whenever they are confronted with what they consider to be a big deal. Even very successful people have this mental block. It is, of course, relative to the person's financial or business position. The man making $100 per week will, in general, consider an expenditure over one thousand dollars to be a big deal. The executive making $25,000 or more per year might consider a $100,000 deal as large. We find men whose mental block doesn't work for less than a million or even ten million dollars, but the block is still there; it just works at different levels for different people.

SECRET WEAPON TO USE IN MASS MARKET SALES

We can depend on this fact: in selling land to the general public, we will be dealing with a large percentage of people who think small and therefore buy small. This is our secret weapon: we think bigger than they do and we act and buy bigger than they do; then we sell small—we sell to fit the mass market. The profit is in the masses. As the old saying goes: sell to the masses, live with the classes.

BUY WHOLESALE, SELL RETAIL

In previous chapters you found out that you are the wholesale buyer and the retail seller; in other words, you buy large and sell small. Now you are learning that the majority of people want to buy small; you are filling the need. Filling a need has always been the basis for business success. With the need defined, we must take the action that will make it possible for us to fill that need and do it on a profitable basis. To fill this need profitably, we must have a product; our product is land. To have land we must either buy the land or in some manner contract to control land.

There are many methods of owning or controlling land. You can pick and choose from these methods. You may even be able to combine or refine some of them. If you are able to develop a new method, you will indeed have the Midas touch in the land business. We are now going to explore a series of methods to put the Think Small Profit Principal to work.

AN EXAMPLE

Here is our project: We are going to find a piece of property consisting of not less than 25 acres and we are going to convert part of it into 75 X 150 foot lots, and part of it into one acre or larger tracts. We will establish our selling price based on our cost for the land, the cost of improvements, such as roads, clearing, etc.; add the cost of the survey, legal fees, etc.; estimate the sales and advertising costs; now, taking this total we find our square foot cost, and then we determine a square foot selling price. Why a square foot basis? Using a square foot basis we can sell any size piece of property, and without difficulty establish our cost basis and our lowest profitable selling price. This is back to our old friend, flexibility. To really deal profitably in land, we must try to retain flexibility—the ability to alter our course of action. The ability to sell what is wanted is the key to dealing in land at a profit.

READY TO PROFIT

We have our land; we know our basic price structure. Referring to the preceding chapters, we have the answers to anticipated questions our prospects may ask. We have the forms and legal contracts to consummate the sale of our property; we are ready to sell on a cash basis or on short-term or long-term credit.

FINDING THE BUYER

As always, we arrive back at the Where do we get the customers and Why should he buy our land question. The answer is always the same in basics, yet may be different in specifics. Each piece of land will appeal to some person or group of persons. People buy desert land, land that is miles from civilization, land that at this time cannot produce any salable product. We learn very early in our study of land this one basic factor—someone will buy any piece of land. A second important fact is that if a person does not want or desire ownership of a specific piece of land, he will in some cases not even accept that land as a gift.

VALUE BASED ON BUYER'S DESIRE

The value of a piece of property is based on the desire in the mind of the buyer for that specific piece of property. Therefore, find the people who most desire the type of property you are offering. This is done through advertising. Advertising covers a variety of techniques. Paid ads in newspapers, trade papers, and magazines are only a part of advertising. Word of mouth advertising can be very effective. Generally speaking, you must start with ads in some mass audience publication. This gets your first customers, then these customers become your unpaid salesmen. You can offer inducements to influence these owners to increase their efforts in telling their friends and relatives about the property you have for sale. You must exercise care that you do not break the laws governing the sale of real estate in your state. Here we come back to our rule that a good lawyer is a must if you deal in land. Advertise to start the motion. Convince the buyer he has made a wise decision. This is action creating more action.

The psychology of thinking small, desiring small should be exploited throughout your sales and advertising campaign. Never, I repeat, *never* use these words or explain to the prospect that he is a small thinker. Remember, this is your secret; share it with your prospect and it is not your secret any more. Share this knowledge of his buy small syndrome with your prospect and you will lose the sale. We are dealing in a fact of life that none of us wants to admit exists in us. Our reluctance to admit that the think small mental block exists does not change the fact that it does exist.

EXAMPLE OF IGNORING THE
THINK SMALL PROFIT PRINCIPLE

The author is involved in a subdivision at this time that proves the Think Small, Buy Small block can be the deadly enemy of success if ignored. This subdivision was started by a group of intelligent, moderately wealthly men. One of these men, a building contractor, had previous experience in subdividing land for home sites. Amazing as it may be, one of these men was a licensed land engineer and surveyor. The other two had not been involved in land development before—one was a doctor, the other a magazine publisher. These four men purchased a 250 acre tract of land on a not yet completed federal reservoir. They spent thousands of dollars clearing the land that would front on the water. More thousands were spent on building a landing strip for small airplanes. Then they subdivided about one-half of this land into very large lots on the waterfront, and medium size tracts of land on the balance. They then registered this subdivision and started offering the property to the public. They sold a few of the waterfront lots to wealthy friends, then their sales program bogged down. One of these men happened to be a friend of mine and he asked me to attend a meeting of the four owners of the property. At this meeting they outlined what they had done and that now they couldn't seem to find buyers for their lots. They offered me an equal share in the ownership corporation in return for my taking over the sale of the property. I agreed to take the plat maps and other information relating to the property and study the situation.

THE THINK SMALL PRINCIPLE
DOOMS THE PROJECT

We now have the elements that have changed a potentially fast profit into a loss, or at best a low, slow profit. If the reader will follow this project carefully, you will first verify the fact that the "think small" mental block does exist and that it is easier to start a project right than to revise a project that is already set up wrong.

We find that here we have a subdivision that to the inexperienced looks perfect. We will now follow the trials and tribulations of these four very intelligent men in their land deal. They ran ads in the proper newspapers; they told their friends about the wonderful lake property available in their subdivision. They sold ten or eleven lots and tracts to their friends, then nothing. They had exhausted their friends as customers. They continued to advertise and sold two or three more lots in a period of about one year. That was when they called me in as a consultant partner-to-be.

EXPERIENCE PLUS TESTING SOLVES
THE SALES PROBLEM

I studied the plat map, ran the mathematics on cost factors, and found that the prices they were asking on a square foot basis were, if anything, not high enough. If they had good land and were not asking more than the market price, why weren't the sales going well? I decided to run a series of tests. I made a tentative agreement that would lead to my having 20 percent of the ownership corporation, then I started my tests. Using the remaining unplatted part of the total property, I subdivided into small 50 X 100 foot lots. (See Exhibit 11-1.) I priced these lots at more per square foot but less per lot than the lots in the adjoining land. Now we had tracts, large lots and small lots. I advertised lots near the lake with starting prices of $199 each. These ads pulled in a considerable number of prospects. I advertised

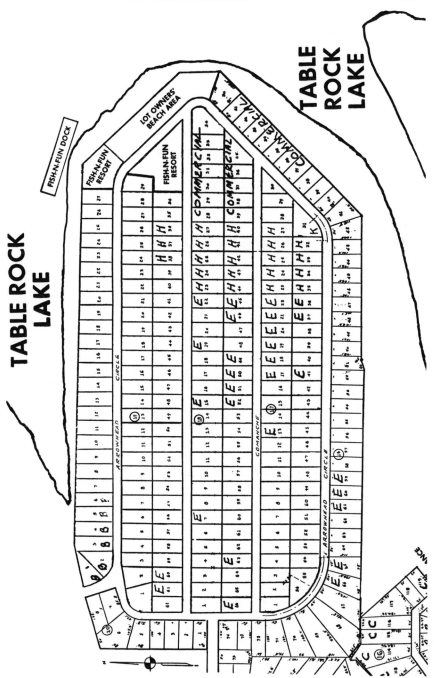

Exhibit 11-1. Subdivision Plat Map

lakefront lots as low as $499. This brought in many more prospects. I then advertised the tracts at $895, which was less than one half the per square foot price on the other lots. In other words, the best buy was the tracts. Yet the results of these tract ads was almost no prospects and absolutely no sales of the tracts. We did sell a number of smaller lots to the prospects we received from our tract advertising. As a result of these tests, I bought the entire acreage on a contract arrangement with the owner corporation. I relinquished my original agreement to be a stockholder in the owner corporation. The situation now was as follows: I had control of the entire 250 acres less the airstrip and certain lots being held by the four original owners and, of course, less the lots already sold. I now had additional areas surveyed into small lots. I concentrated my advertising on these lots. In the first year I sold over 200 of these lots at square foot prices higher than the prices on the large lots and tracts. Taking advantage of the desire of most people to buy small, this project was converted into a very profitable deal.

APPLY A PROFIT FACT NOT A THEORY

Buying, preparing, and selling in the land business requires study, planning, and testing. We have just followed the results of not knowing how to plan. You have also seen in an actual development sales operation that the think small, buy small syndrome can be a deadly enemy of the land developer when this fact of life is ignored. I can't emphasize too strongly that we are involved with a psychological fact, a fact that can be depended on to be true now and always. This is not a theory; I repeat—it is a proven fact.

PUT THE THINK SMALL SYNDROME TO WORK

1. Buy a fairly large piece of land
2. Buy it wholesale
3. Divide the land into smaller pieces
4. Advertise these pieces for sale to the general public
5. Sell at retail

If you do this, you cannot fail to make a profit. The demand for small pieces of land is so great as to almost guarantee your sales.

By applying the sales psychology inherent in the "Think Small, Buy Small" Syndrome in almost any land venture, you will install your own profit fail-safe.

Remember, you are dealing with psychological fact. The majority of people do think and buy small. This one fact, when properly applied, can make your fortune in land.

12

Buy Now--Pay Later
for Fast Profits

Time payments—the bane of our lives or the boon to our business. Some companies make more profits from their time charges than they make from the sale of the merchandise. The English call time payments the "Never Never Plan," and the way some people use credit they never, never get out of debt.

CREDIT A WAY OF LIFE

There is, however, an amazing side to the use of credit. Many families are raised, the children given good educations and the family has a wonderful life, all paid for through the proper use of credit. Being in debt no longer has any social stigma. It is an historical fact that less than fifty years ago the use of credit for luxury items was considered by many people to be a form of immorality. In fact, up until the 1930's the purchase on credit of anything other than a home was not only considered immoral, it was considered a form of stupidity. If you wanted a car or furniture, etc., you saved your money until you had the cash and then you bought the item.

Credit was the exception, credit cards unheard of, and the fact of being in debt was to be concealed from your friends and relatives. Your friendly banker wasn't so friendly, and his bank more nearly resembled a jail than a place of business. Interest rates were low; collateral requirements high. Your personal reputation and financial background needed to be so good that the old story—if you were rich enough to get a loan you didn't need one—was more true than can be believed today.

THIS IS THE CREDIT AGE

We live in the time and age where we are besieged with offers of credit, credit, and more credit. Any person who has not up to this time abused his credit could, if he so desired, buy thousands and thousands of dollars worth of things without one dime in cash. This person would probably have more than a little trouble paying the bills that would result. The important fact is that this person could get such a large amount of goods, merchandise, and even cash, all on credit. It would be possible, for example, to buy two, three, or four cars, a boat, clothing, furniture, etc. Add a series of credit cards to just regular credit and the amount of credit readily available is staggering.

MOST CREDIT BUYERS ARE HONEST

Only the good sense of most Americans has kept this easy credit situation from becoming a catastrophe. Most Americans are not only intelligent but they are honest and they do pay their bills, even if it hurts. I have lost very little money in real estate due to dishonesty. I have lost some money in dealing with people who became ill, lost their job, or just plain overbought. Credit is valuable to each one of us. We all will be involved in its use in some manner. It is a wonderful tool, if used with care.

CREDIT IS THE LAND DEALER'S BEST FRIEND

I would not have been able to deal in land on any major scale without the use of credit. My first speculative land venture was the purchase of a large tract of land for $14,000 with a $4,000 down payment. (See Exhibit 12-1.) You will be looking at the subdivision that resulted from that $4,000 down payment. You can do your own arithmetic to estimate the dollar sales in such a subdivision. You, the land buyer, will most probably want and

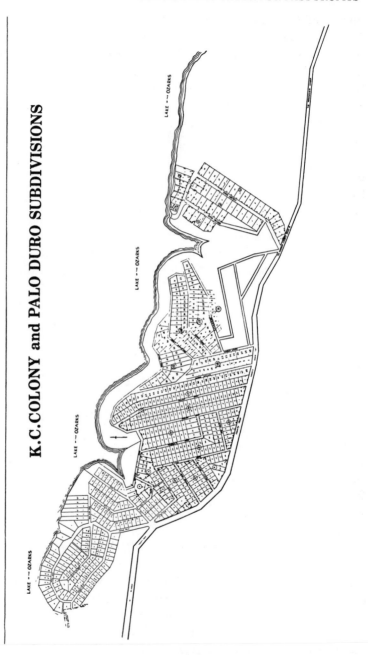

Courtesy of Kirk C. Colony of Ozarks, Inc., Kansas City, Missouri

Exhibit 12-1. Plat Map of Large Tract

need credit. You can gain such favorable leverage with credit that $1 can do the work of $5, $10, even $100. This multiplies your profits and makes credit a member of your investment team. To make selling your property at a profit as easy as possible we must buy right. Credit money leverage may be the secret of your buying right. If you can purchase 250, 500, or 1,000 acres instead of 25, 50 or 100 acres, you should have the following advantages: The per acre price will be substantially lower. It is cheaper per acre to develop a large tract than a small one. Once you get your sales going you don't run out of product. As you sell more and more lots you can generally raise prices as the area develops. The more land you start with, the more of this area increase in value will come to you. Let's use an example.

AN EXAMPLE OF CREDIT BUYING

A farmer has a 720 acre farm. You determine that you could convert this into lots and small tracts. You would need to increase the size of a small existing lake. You have located a place that would be easy to dam and to make a second small lake. You have checked out the highway and road situation. You approach the farmer on the basis of buying a parcel of 100 acres. You will almost always find either he doesn't want to sell part of his farm or, if he is willing to sell a part, his per acre price will be very high. The best arrangement is to buy the entire farm. Get his lowest price per acre. Then make him an offer at his per acre price, but on your terms. In many cases you can afford to pay 10 percent to 20 percent more per acre if you get the kind of terms that allows you to obtain control over the entire acreage. Here you are using your credit to put yourself in the land business on the best basis for present and future profits.

The seller will in most instances finance the sale himself. He is only too glad to sell at a satisfactory per acre price and then make extra money from interest on the unpaid balance.

You are in a sense buying on the same basis you will be selling. The important difference is that you are buying wholesale, but you will be selling retail.

You buy on credit; later you sell on credit. The income from your credit sales will make the payments on your credit purchase.

Your customers will in fact make your payments and as your sales develop, give you a substantial profit.

YOUR REPUTATION MAKES OBTAINING
CREDIT EASY

You will find that a good reputation will make land deals much easier. My best boosters are the people I have bought from and the people I have sold to. When you are dealing on credit, a good reputation is the same as money.

I have had people say: take over the land; pay us when you get the sales started; we know how you dealt with Mr. So and so and we trust you. I would then put the deal in writing, but with no down payment and a clause giving me extra time on the payments. Then I would proceed to do a good job for myself and keep my word to the seller. In dealing in land, your reputation can act as money. You can get road builders, surveyors, etc., to work with you on a percentage of the sales or just wait until you get your sales going before you pay them. You can buy that extra acreage if terms are available. Your reputation can make terms available. Here your reputation can and will make no cash deals in land possible.

KEEP YOUR PROMISES

A reputation of this calibre is hard to earn and easy to lose. Promise only what you can do and do what you promise. The successful life must be one of honor and integrity. In business, whether real estate or other, a reputation for integrity is money in the bank.

CREDIT SELLING IN ACTION

First, we know that this country is set up to do all types of business on credit. We know we can buy and sell on time payments. We know that we expect to pay interest when we use credit to buy. We know that we can charge interest when we sell on credit. The best thing we know is that our prospect will, as a general rule, buy more if credit is available. This fact increases the salability of our land and will in most cases increase the price per square foot we can charge for the land. Combine the increased amount of sales with a higher selling price, then add the interest we can charge for the time payment plan, and you begin to see that the use of credit can be the gateway to the profit promise land.

EXAMPLE OF THE EXTRA PROFIT

Let's trace an actual sale of one lot in a subdivision. Cost factor in this lot is estimated at $200. Selling price desired is $695. We will sell for $595 cash, or $695 on time payments.

Here are the mathematics of this sale:

Sale Price	$695
Less down payment	− 95
Balance to carry on credit	$600
*Time charge of 6 percent	140
Total amount	$740

Payable in 48 monthly payments of $17.50 per month, plus taxes. Tax estimates on this vacant lot, $8.00 per year. (Remember, vacant land carries the lowest tax base of any real estate).

Now let us review the profit on this transaction. Our estimated costs, including land, roads, surveys, legal, advertising, and sales expenses was $200. Our total return is $740 in payments plus $95 as down payment, or a total of $835; deduct our $200 cost basis and we have a profit of $635; this is over 300 percent return on our investment. We will, over a period of four years, receive a return of more than four times the cost of the land, including all expenses. This is 100 percent per year. It is obvious that you can't go to the poor farm on deals such as this.

We can easily raise or lower the figures involved. I sometimes sell lots for very little more than the cost basis. Other times I sell

---

*Time charge is based on 6 percent add on interest for four years. Add on interest is computed as follows: $600 at 6% = $600 x .06% = $36 per year, multiplied by four years = $144 in interest referred to as time charge. We have rounded the interest charge figure to $140 to make payment come out to an even $17.50 per month.

for 5-10-20-100 times cost basis. I have never sold any land for less than cost basis. I have never had any land that I couldn't sell to someone for at least a small profit.

CREDIT INCREASES SALES

We have followed the profit potential in selling a lot on time payments. We can readily see that this profitability is excellent. Now an even more important fact: The lot in question might have stayed unsold for a much longer time and then been sold at a much lower price if we had not sold on terms. The author has at times offered lots on a cash only basis. This was done to raise operating money. It has been a source of amazement to me that the following is a fact. A prospect would not buy a certain lot for $250 cash; he would pay $500 for this same lot if he could pay $50 down and $15 per month. The prospect would not only pay double the price, he would also pay the interest charge. There are some people who buy for cash. They, as a rule, drive a pretty hard bargain. I have sold hundreds of lots and small tracts to cash buyers. These cash buyers can be a big help when you need some quick cash in your pocket or quick operating money. You must be prepared in general to make less profit when you sell to these buyers. Our old friend flexibility is back—be flexible, be able to sell for cash or terms. Be able to deal with the prospect in the manner that will convert him from prospect to buyer.

THE LAND DEALER'S ANNUITY PLAN

The buildup of a substantial number of buyers paying you on a monthly installment plan can result in a large amount of income per month. This income continues long after the sales effort was made. This type arrangement can become a form of annuity. You have the land bought, improved, paid for and sold, yet for years, without any action on your part, you receive income. This can be pre-planned for an income program for your less active older years. The author has reached the stage where he is introducing some younger persons into his operation. They will work with some of the land that the author has acquired using the "Sell

Some–Hold Some" method. These young men, under the author's guidance, can make money for themselves and make money for the author. The margin of profit is large enough in most good land operations that the dealer can allow participation. I am training these people to use the methods that are explained in this book. I am putting extra emphasis on credit selling. The reason for the emphasis on credit selling is based on the fact that we live and do business in a credit environment. Credit is one of today's most powerful selling tools if understood and used in a proper manner.

TEST AND RETEST FOR MOST PROFIT

How to make credit sell your property. Here we must again consider our advertising. Should we sell on total price, down payment, monthly payment, or all three? Back to our test theory: test the market. Let the customers answer our questions. A simple test can be conducted as follows: Each weekend for three weekends we will advertise the same lots. First weekend we offer our lots with the biggest copy being total price for lowest priced lot with notation that they can be bought with a small down payment and terms. The next weekend we advertise with the down payment being the dominant figure. We offer our lowest priced lot for so much down. This should be the lowest down payment we will accept. Do not mention total price or amount of monthly payments. The third weekend we advertise with the monthly payment as the dominant figure. We do not mention the down payment or the total amount. Variants of these three ads can also be tested, such as showing down payment, monthly payments, and even total amount in the same ad. Stress quality and usefulness of property, mention long range value increase! Now evaluate actual prospects and sales generated by each ad. Maybe you will want to use all of them over again. Maybe one will do a so much better sales job that you will use it exclusively for a time. This is the only way even a professional advertising man can really check the market. It is still the ad that sells; that is, the good ad. Pretty ads, ads that sound good, may or may not sell. Your only yardstick is the results.

CREDIT SELLS IF YOU TELL

Use the time payment plan to sell your property. You can only do this if people know what you have to sell and on what terms. The time payment plan will work for you only if the prospects know it's available. You have a good product, priced right, and now with your time payment plan you can make it available to almost anyone who really wants to buy. You have the combination that always works. You must be sure that you have all of the above in your land project, then you must be sure that as many people know about it as possible. Don't keep it a secret; you have something to sell—sell it. If you tell your friends, neighbors, relatives, advertise in newspapers, put signs on the property, then credit will help sell your properties. Credit sells land—don't keep its availability a secret from your prospects.

Here is the secret—don't keep it a secret.

SPECIAL NOTE

In selling land on terms using some form of contract for deed, you do not need to spend time or money checking the buyer's credit. Remember you do not deliver the title to the property until all the payments have been made. You give only possession, not ownership, during the payment period. If the buyer does not make payments as per his contract for deed, he loses the money he has paid and you, the seller, still have clear title to the land.

It is a simple matter to default and resell land sold using the land contract or contract for deed. You can avoid the unpleasant task of pressuring persons who are in default on their payments. You write them, explaining that they are behind in their payments. You give them a certain period of time, such as thirty days, to bring their payments up to date. If they do not take such action within their allotted time period, I send them a registered letter giving them thirty days to pay their complete balance.

If they do not respond to the registered letter, I put the property back on the market and resell it.

RECAP CREDIT

1. Credit is a way of life for most people.
2. Most credit buyers are honest.
3. Credit selling makes many more sales possible.
4. Credit selling makes sales at a higher, more profitable price possible.
5. Credit selling adds extra profit from the interest charged.
6. Credit selling creates a cash income spread over an extended period of time.
7. Credit selling spreads your income over more than one year, thus reducing the amount of income tax liability.

Examine these facts–you have more sales at higher prices plus a profit from the interest charged, and you pay less taxes. This adds up to more money in your pocket.

All of this extra profit and income is the direct result of selling land on credit.

Your fortune in land may be based on your using credit both when you buy and when you sell. Credit properly used is the land dealer's best friend–use it.

Special note: Check the Truth in Lending law to determine its applicability to your operation.

13

How to Create Value and Put Money in Your Pocket

Sit very still in a bathtub filled with water—sit very, very still. Don't move—watch the water; it will be still, placid, motionless. Now move your hand in the water: as your hand moves, so does the water, and the water moves not just around your hand but all over the area of the tub. Move your hand faster and the water starts to create waves, and if you are not careful the water will splash over the sides onto the floor. This may seem childish, but it will not seem so childish if you get the impact of "Motion Creating Motion" and how it spreads out from the source in an ever-increasing area. Move and you have movement, push and you start something moving. Act and you create action. The younger generation has a saying about being where the action is. It is a fact that not only the young but the majority of the people want to be where the action is.

PEOPLE RELAX THROUGH ACTION

It's almost ridiculous to hear people plan on a vacation to rest—relax—get away from it all. Then where do they go? Records show they go to New York City, Las Vegas, Acapulco, London, Paris, Rome, Rio—get away from what? I'll tell you what they get away from: their routine and their responsibilities. They do this through action—even when they sit—they want to sit and watch people or the ocean or something that moves. They watch action. TV is action enjoyed passively. The most popular shows are loaded with action. So believe it or not, you are a member of the action set. You, if you are average, are not a loner, you are not a sitter for very long periods—you want, crave, need, and demand people, change, action, motion.

SELL ACTION

The dealer in land recognizes that even when he is selling a piece of property in the country he must sell action. This land is only so many minutes to the store, theatre, bowling alley, bar, etc. People seem to contradict themselves with the getting away from it all story. A prospect will buy land miles from people and then spend a great deal of time driving to the places where the people are.

The land dealer is first of all an action person. Second, the land dealer recognizes the need for action in his potential buyers. Here we find that if you use the action-creating profit principal you will negate the need for you to be a good salesman. The things you show about the use of your land will do your selling—you create the value.

URBAN EXAMPLE

A simple piece of unimproved property is located at the edge of a medium-size city—value, $10,000 to $12,000; present use, none. Here is a piece of land at its lowest value point, bringing in no income—it is ripe for two types of use by the dealer in land. Purchase for long-range price increase. Situated as it is, time and population explosion will most surely increase the value of this property in the years to come. The small tax cost would be a negligible factor. So we have a long-term profit potential opportunity. The second use would be to put the Value Creating Profit Principle into action. Act and create value.

HOW TO CREATE VALUE?

The question is, how can this be done? First, we examine all the potentials of this property. Start with location, then surroundings, then area needs. If this property were located on a main street or a major highway, then it would be easy. Generally, we will not find property at the edge of town on main streets and highways available at reasonable prices. It is too easy for the local real estate men to visualize the uses of that type of property. The property we are talking about is generally off the main trafficway one or two blocks. We find we can get this property zoned for small business, office building, or a combination of the two. Now we have a base to start action.

OPTION IF POSSIBLE

If possible, obtain an option on this land, and if possible, without any appreciable amount of cash. That is action one: it will cause ripples; the word will spread; the "what's going on, why does this buyer want the option, what does he know," gossip can increase land values. You are not going to trade on this, you are going to create real action. You now approach local doctors and dentists on the basis of their building a small medical building. At the same time you approach lawyers and accountants about a building to house lawyers and accountants. This is a natural grouping, as one can help the other to get business. In your spare time you write letters to franchise companies in the laundromat, pizza parlor, etc., type of operations. Now we have the action going strong. Now we start getting the reaction; now the prospects start coming to us.

SPEND SOME OF YOUR TIME ON DETAILS

We may add to the action with ads in the paper or letters to local business people outlining all or certain of the possibilities of this property. Work up detailed proposals for the most obvious uses of this property—estimated costs for different types of buildings, projected returns from different uses. Show how a small combine of men can convert this property into a profitable investment by building a building to rent or lease. Think of many uses; remember, you can conceive these uses at no cost to you.

You are dealing only in the land; sell the use—let the buyers do the building. You are interested in profiting from the land. To do this you must study the possiblities.

You also must be certain you can furnish title insurance when you sell. The need for title insurance in this deal is so that your buyers will not have a title problem when they go to get their financing.

FINANCING CAN MAKE THE DEAL

Help the prospects locate financing. In some cases you may be able to participate in the financing. In general, your buyers will need clear title to the land before they can get a loan for construction. This means you will, in most deals of this nature, be paid in cash.

However, you may wish to participate in the financing: you can do this at no risk to yourself. If you paid $12,000 for the land and you now sell it for $25,000 as the site for the medical building, you can take $12,000 in cash, using this to pay your entire cost and deliver a clear mortgage-free title. Take personal notes from the investors for the balance of $13,000 with interest and have each one of these investors sign individually and personally to guarantee the payments to you. This way you will make your profit plus the interest. If the principals are men of good character and reasonable financial background you have a note that can be used as collateral to raise additional cash when you need it. By helping finance the land you reduce the amount of cash the investors need to raise to build their building. Here you have made additional profit and helped make the deal possible. This is another action creating an action, creating profit and more profit. This is you creating value.

YES, THE DEALER IN LAND
CAN MAKE SUCH DEALS

This may seem to you to be oversimplified. You may say, "Is such a deal really possible?" The answer is that land deals like the one described are being consummated every day. You must recognize that the dealer in land does the things that most people don't even know can be done. Ask yourself if you know how to make a nuclear reactor. Unless you are one in a million, the answer is no. Yet to the men who know how to make a nuclear reactor it is no mystery. They merely put into action certain laws of physics and nature to achieve a predetermined result.

You are becoming the one in a million in dealing in land. You are learning the laws that govern action and reaction. You are learning the facts of life as they pertain to this one field of endeavor. The rewards of your study and work can build your *fortune in land.*

PROFITS ARE NOT MIRACLES

The purchase of a small piece of urban property for $12,000 and its ultimate sale for $25,000 is not a miracle. It was the result of the efforts of the dealer in land. If you create a desire in someone for a certain piece of land, this will increase its value. You create this desire by showing how this person or persons can profit in either pleasure or money through their ownership and use of this land. You can see that this is a formula based on sound business principles and basic logic. You, the land dealer, fill a need; more than that, by your action, you create a need. Here is action creating action, and action creating value.

ACTION CREATES PROFITS FROM
COUNTRY PROPERTY

This same action principle can be applied to country property. The same basic formula can convert unused, rough, country land into an enjoyable and profitable real estate operation. Here we start with a substandard farm and change it into a money-making, exciting place for people to use. Here we create the country retreat and retirement area that is so much in demand. Using your own efforts, your know-how, and your planning you create value, you create action, you create profits. Now let's examine the details of how to start this action.

WORST FARM?

First, select the worst farm, on the best road, near a substantial population source. Now buy this farm for the least money, with the best terms you can get. There are two reasons for looking for the worst farm. It will, number one, be much lower in price per acre than a good farm; and two, believe it or not it will in general be better for your purpose. The worst land for farming is often the best for resale as lots for homesites or small tracts for that "get away to the country place" that so many people want. Such a farm generally has rough terrain, it is wooded, it is natural—and these things make this land beautiful to the eye. It, however, does not lend itself to profitable farming. You will find many such marginal farms if you follow the how to buy land information in this book. To recapitulate at this time, watch the advertisements in the classified section of local newspapers. Let the suburban and farm real estate dealers know you are looking for this type of property. Here is a word of caution. Do not take the real estate dealers into your confidence. It is not necessary that they know your plans for the property they are helping you find. All they need to know is that you are interested in buying a cheap farm.

SALES PLAN CREATES ACTIONS AND PROFITS

Once you have purchased the property that meets your requirements you are ready to start your action. Examine the land to determine the easiest way to start an initial income flow. Is there a lake or pond that can be stocked for fishing? Can it be enlarged so as to offer even limited boating? Is there a place on the property that can be dammed so an artificial lake can be created? Even a very small lake can be the key to increased profits. The government published a booklet on farm ponds that can be of real help in knowing where and how to create what we will call a series of miniature lakes.

Next select natural building sites—knolls that overlook the surrounding land. A stream or even a ravine can be used to create interesting and attractive building sites. You can always sell the flat land. The key is to get the most from the choice land and the most from the poorest quality land. It seems odd that you may devote a great deal of time and thought to the worst of your property. That is the land that creative planning can change from waste to profit. The key to profit is to use all of your land in the best manner possible.

LEARN FROM YOUR PROSPECTS

Plan your property, then test. Let the reactions of your prospects and customers tell you what action you should take. Here is a simple test that can be used prior to your spending any money on improvements or survey. Place an ad in the classified section of the paper in the city nearest your land. Your ad will read, "Beautiful Country building sites, $495 up, low down payment, easy terms, call Mr. Jones AR5-9762." This ad invites people interested in a beautiful country place at a reasonable price and on easy terms to call you. When the prospect calls, you explain in as much detail as possible, giving location, road conditions, driving time, and other pertinent data. Then explain the wide choice of different type building sites available. Stress beauty of land along with price and terms. Here we find our old friend, Mr. Flexible. You offer selection, price, terms. You do not say take what we have—you say what do you want.

YOUR FIRST CUSTOMER ACTION

From these calls you will find those who are really interested in your type property. This will create your first customer action. Now arrange meetings with these prospects to see the property. It can be good psychology to show as many prospects as possible on the same day, even at the same time. This saves your time and money, plus it is good sales psychology.

As we have said before, people like to be where the action is. When one prospect sees that other people are interested in buying your property, they seem to feel that this must be a good deal. It seems that if a total stranger is willing to take a certain action, we are more willing to take that same action. The logic of this may escape us; the fact that we do play follow the leader is true. You can sell more property when your prospects are aware of the actions of your other prospects. Let the word spread that this is where the action is and you will find that your property is in demand.

ACTION CREATES CONTINUING ACTION

By this time your initial action is creating some sales. Now your next action will be based on a careful evaluation of this first phase; you have talked to the prospect who bought and talked to the prospect who didn't buy. Why did one buy and why didn't the other one buy? The answers to the *why* and *why not* should give you most of the answers as to how to proceed in developing this property. In addition to these answers, you have also obtained a flow of income from your initial sales. You can now afford to make the improvements, complete your needed surveys, and do other things such as building and/or stocking the lake. Here we are using other people's money to increase the value and salability of our property.

You should always strive to hold your investment to the smallest amount needed to get the job done. It is easy to overspend and even easier to overextend your credit. Move with care and remember—plan, test, act.

SECOND PHASE

You have now reached the second phase of your action plan for your country property. You must now be certain that the property you sold as a result of your first test ads is properly and legally surveyed. As you used a metes and bounds survey to determine the lots or tracts you sold, you must now have a legal description and a plat map made by a licensed surveying engineer of each lot, tract, or parcel of land sold. This is very easy and any surveyor can do the job. This will make it possible for you to deliver title to those purchasers paying cash. The customers who bought on terms should have signed a contract for deed form and you will need the proper legal description to show exactly what they are paying for.

Here we see that with ownership of the land we can advertise and sell lots, tracts, and parcels of this property prior to an actual survey of these pieces of land. Let the customer decide what he wants, where he wants it, and as long as that selection does not interfere with your general plan for the entire property, you can and are happy to sell him his heart's desire. You, of course, have determined your square foot costs, including the costs of yet to be done surveys and improvements. All that is needed is a customer willing to pay the price per square foot that will make you the profit you want.

Your customer is now the action agent—he is creating your action; you are benefiting from his desires and his action. This is the motion creates motion theory creating sales.

A $127,300 PROFIT

You will find it interesting to pursue a hypothetical country land project from the profit standpoint:

Land costs—180 acres @ $125.00 per acre =	$22,500
Actual cash paid out	
(Down payment)	$2,500
Cost of advertising, building, lake, roads,	
surveying, and miscellaneous	$10,600
Interest on unpaid balance	5,200
Total Costs (not including land)	$15,800
We now have land cost	$22,500
Interest Costs	5,200
Land & Interest Cost	$27,700
Actual cash outlay to start project	$ 2,500
We figure our cost per acre is approximately	$ 164
43,500 square feet per acre gives us a per	
square foot cost	.0037

You can therefore sell a building site 75 X 150 ft. for $199 and this results in a profit of $157 based on a cost of $42. On this basis the entire property will bring in $155,000 gross, or a profit not including interest income of $127,300. It is possible, if enough cash sales or cash flow can be generated, that very little actual cash over the $2,500 down payment will be needed. You should, however, plan on investing about $5,000 cash in a deal of this size.

JOINT VENTURE

This type land project can be perfect for two, three, or more participants to join with the land dealer. You, the dealer, can put such a project together and retain 50 percent of it and not put up any of the capital. Your contribution is the know-how and the doing. Here is where your action can be your only investment. This puts you in an all-win—no-loss position. Never get other people into a land deal unless you are very sure it will be profitable for them. Your reputation is on the line every time you do business.

You can make this type of deal using as few as twenty acres—the method is the same. The return percentage will generally be lower on the smaller deal.

Generally, when you buy a substandard farm, you will get a substandard farmhouse and/or barn or two, and maybe a chicken house. This can be a little gravy in the deal. If you are a handyman, you might want to fix it up for your operating base and then sell it when all the land is sold, or you might just sell it to a handy-man type. Any way you do it, it is all profit.

THINK, CREATE, ACT AND PROFIT

Now you have seen how the dealer in land can, by his actions, create profits. Here is your opportunity to use your time and talents to be the action man. You can actually make huge profits through creative action, and you can start doing it now.

VALUE CREATING IN ACTION

Mr. E.T. a real spare time pro. Mr. E.T. is a spare time dealer in land. Mr. E.T. is also a professional in land development. Mr. E.T. is a contractor and builder of homes, apartments, and townhouses. He buys urban and surburban land as part of his everyday business. Then Mr. E.T. deals in resort land as his spare time fortune builder.

Mr. E.T. knows land and its uses. In his spare time Mr. E.T. buys, sells, and enjoys resort land. You may be wondering about this enjoys part. Mr. E.T. is a pilot, a hunter, a fisherman, and a boating enthusiast. Through his spare time dealing in resort property Mr. E.T. owns land on lakes: these lands are in areas of fine fishing, hunting, and boating. Mr. E.T. has an airstrip on one of these properties. Mr. E.T. flies to his spare time land deal, goes hunting, fishing, boating, and sells some property as he does all these things.

Mr. E.T. enjoys and profits from his spare time land deals. Mr. E.T. is healthier, happier, and richer, plus he spends his weekends making a profit from doing the things he loves to do. That is most certainly enjoying your investment.

Mr. R.R. Controls His Annual Income—by controlling his annual land sales, Mr. R.R. controls his income at a preselected level. A few years ago Mr. R.R. decided he wanted to be able to spend more time enjoying life and less time working. Mr. R.R. made a plan based on his love of the outdoors and of fishing.

Mr. R.R. bought from his savings and earnings a large tract of land in the country near a lake. During a period of five years he built a home for himself and his family and started to implement his plan.

Mr. R.R. subdivided a portion of his land; he built roads as required, but only in this subdivided area. He then cleared, cleaned, and made beautiful a number of these lots. In some cases he put split rail fences and other decorative items to make these lots look attractive.

Mr. R.R. was now able to sell these lots for top dollar. Mr. R.R. established a price per lot that gave him a very substantial profit. Mr. R.R. did most of his own financing.

Mr. R.R. set a figure of $25,000 per year personal income. When sales reach the amount that will give Mr. R.R. his $25,000 profit, he simply stops selling.

Based on the amount of land Mr. R.R. owns, he can at the present profit margin have this $25,000 annual income for the balance of his life and still leave land to his children.

Mr. R.R. has accomplished this by using the method that is explained in detail in this book.

1. Buy well-selected land in an area where you want to deal.

2. Buy it wholesale and on terms you can handle.

3. Sell retail by selling smaller tracts or lots to fill the need of most people for a small piece of land.

4. You can pay for the land from its income because you are making your living from your regular income source.

5. Having a large portion of this land paid for when you retire and thereby having a substantial income from sales each year during retirement.

Mr. R.R. wanted early retirement, he wanted to live in the country, and he liked to fish.

Mr. R.R. was able to have all these things with financial security as a result of his land deal. What Mr. R.R. did others are doing, and so can you.

14

Mail Order Selling:
Money in Your Mailbox

Without doubt, mail order selling is one of the perfect ways to operate as a dealer in land. Here is the sales method that puts the United States Post Office on your sales team. You and the mailman can sell to hundreds, even thousands of people. These people can be spread over wide areas of our country, yet they are as close as your mailbox.

Here is the best part: using the mail, you can sell to all of these people and never leave your home. Selling by mail in your living room, using your evenings, weekends, or whatever time you have available. Your customer isn't interested in where you are or what time of the day or day of the week you fill his order. Your customer is only interested in buying a good product at a fair price and on the right terms.

EVERY DAY IS PAYDAY

Open your mail and count the money. Yes, once you have established your mail order land business, every mail delivery can be money in your pocket. Imagine your mail bringing in hundreds, even thousands of dollars each week. Now imagine this going on for many years. Even after you quit the active sale of land, the money continues to arrive. Selling by mail on terms will result in your establishing an annuity-type income. This spread of income also reduces your income tax liability. You combine profits and tax shelter with income for your future.

TEN RULES OF MAIL ORDER SELLING

Mail order selling is a specialized field. It requires specialized knowledge and the following of certain basic rules.

1. The product must be suited to sale by mail.
2. The price must be attractive on a competitive basis.
3. The product must have a wide appeal to the mass market.
4. Terms must be available on the higher priced products.
5. A strong sales appeal must be made in a believable manner.
6. The benefits to the buyer must be repeated often.
7. It must be easy for the prospect to make the purchase.
8. You must deliver a good product.
9. The orders must be filled quickly, efficiently, and correctly.
10. An ironclad money back guarantee must assure and protect the buyer.

THE MAIL ORDER METHOD

In this chapter you will learn the details of selling land by mail. We will deal primarily with resort-type property, as this type of land lends itself best to sale by mail. You will learn the methods that have and are being used with great success all over our country. Most important, you will learn how to apply these methods yourself. As you learn more, you will find that selling land by mail can be both a pleasure and a profit.

YOUR REPUTATION IS YOUR FUTURE

Now, point one, you must deliver a good product. Do not waste your time and money in mail order selling until you have a good product to sell. Anyone can advertise and offer a poor product by mail. Through the use of misleading advertising a poor product can sound like a good product. Avoid such advertising at all costs.

No one can build a permanent, profitable mail order business based on dishonesty or fraud. Such activities are not only illegal, they are also poor business. Your reputation is always important. In selling by mail, your reputation is your future success or failure. To recap, to sell successfully by mail, you must deliver a good product at a fair price and generally on easy terms.

THE METHOD SELECTS THE LAND

In selling land by mail, you must constantly keep your method of selling in mind as you select the land you will offer. If you intend to establish a continuous business in the selling of land by mail, your purchase must meet certain criteria.

In general mail order, land should be suitable for recreation or retirement or both. Such land should be near, on, or have a body of water involved. Natural beauty, recreational facilities, good access by road, plus modern utilities are all important items.

BUY THE RIGHT LAND

Follow the methods outlined in the chapters on WHERE, WHEN, WHY and HOW to buy. Knowing the sales method you will use will give you the key to what is the right land. Tests can be conducted even before you make your final commitment to buy any land. Remember, plan and test are key elements in a safe, profitable land investment. Nowhere is the plan and test technique easier to put in practice than in selling land by mail. You can virtually eliminate the chance of appreciable loss if you follow the methods outlined in this book.

MAIL ORDER SELLING FACTS

Here are some important facts about mail order land and mail order land customers. More land is sold and more profits are made from land near but not fronting on water. Why is this true? First, land that actually fronts on water is very expensive. Second, good waterfront land is in limited supply, as much of the available water frontage is rough, hilly, and unsuitable for good building sites. Accept this fact: more profit is being made in resort property selling land near the water than is being made selling waterfront land. This is a dependable fact, yet most people believe just the opposite. This makes this knowledge your profit principal.

In setting up your mail order land operation, do the following. Buy one good piece of waterfront property. This land will be used as a waterfront access and recreational area. You can put picnic tables, ovens, water supply, rest rooms, boat and swimming docks on this property. You also buy a large amount of land back from but adjoining this water front land. For a very good example see the Miramar Estates plat. (See Exhibit 14-1.) You offer your prospects perpetual use of this waterfront access and park area. Now you are offering the enjoyment of the water at a price the mass market can afford. Another of your profit principles is in selling the mass market what it wants at a price it can and will pay.

SUBDIVIDE FOR MAXIMUM PROFITS

The manner in which you subdivide your land will be a major determining factor in your profit ratio. Take a very careful look at the plat map of Miramar Estates. (See Exhibit 14-1.) Note the uniformity of the lot sizes. Over 80 percent of the lots in this subdivision are 50 ft. X 100 ft. This results in a usable size, yet it yields a substantial number of lots per acre. Here we apply the square foot cost to square foot selling price. The square foot cost and pricing method gives you your best profit control information. When you know your square foot cost, the determination of a profitable selling price becomes a simple process of mathematics.

PROOF OF PROFIT TO SIZE RELATIONSHIP

Example of size to profit relationship. If the lots in Miramar Estates were 75 X 100 feet, the selling price of each lot would have to be increased by 50 percent to result in the same per dollar of sale profit. If these lots were 50 X 200 feet, it would be necessary to double the price to arrive at approximately the same square foot profit.

CUSTOMERS BUY MORE SMALL LOTS

Lots 50 X 100 feet in size allow the customer to buy the amount of land he wants. He can buy two, three, four or more lots

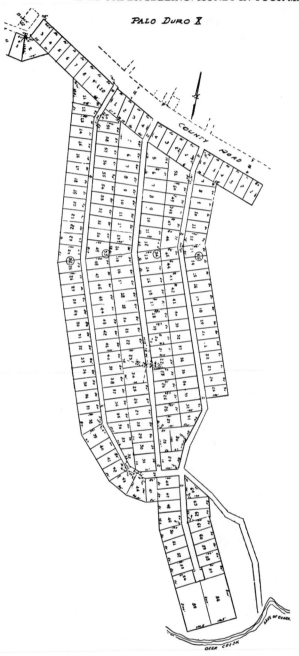

Courtesy of Kirk C. Colony of Ozarks, Inc., Kansas City, Missouri

Exhibit 14-1. Miramar Estates Plat Map

together. Using the purchase of many smaller lots, the customer controls his land costs, he controls his dollar expenditure, and he feels that he is getting more for his money. It sounds more impressive to say he owns four lots than to say he owns one or two, even though the actual amount of land might be the same.

SPECIAL NOTE REGARDING LOT SIZE

There is seldom a reason to make any lot exceptionally deep in relation to its width. Lot size 50 feet front width by 200, 300 or 400 feet deep are in general a great waste of land. Only in rare cases where the terrain is the determining factor is this type lot made available. Buyers are much more interested in width than in depth. In almost all cases a 50 X 100 foot lot will sell for as much money and sell just as easily as a 50 X 150 foot lot. You can readily see that the profit margin will be much better on the 50 X 100 foot lot. To really visualize the reasoning behind this important lot size profit principle, do the following. Make a scale drawing of a 50 X 100 foot lot and a scale drawing of a 50 X 150 foot lot. Now place a scale-drawn rectangle about the size of an average cottage or small house on the two drawings. You quickly see that all the extra 50 feet depth has done is to give the buyers more backyard. Many people mentally convert this extra backyard into more caretaker-type yard work and really would rather not have it.

THE MAIL ORDER SUBDIVISION IN ACTION

Using the information in this book, you purchase property you are sure can be sold by mail. You then subdivide a portion of this property based on the best use of the terrain and the best lot size to profit relationship.

Keeping in mind that your mail order customer is going to verify his decision to buy, you do the following:

1. Supply an easy to follow map to the property.
2. Supply an easy to understand plat map designed so you can clearly indicate lot or lots allocated to the mail order buyer.
3. Install direction signs on roads leading to your subdivision.

You can obtain permission to put the signs on property along the road. You contact the property owners and pay them a small annual fee.

4. Install entrance signs at the road you have decided to use as your main entrance. These signs should be easy to see, easy to read, and kept neat and clean.

5. Have each lot clearly marked with white stakes on all fouɪ corners.

6. Place a small sign at the center of the front line of each lot. This sign will have the lot and block numbers and the name of the subdivision; it can also have price and terms.

7. All signs should have either your name, address and phone number, or that of the person who is your representative.

8. Be sure all roads in the subdivision are in as good condition as possible prior to the start of the advertising sales program.

9. Have someone available at specified times to show lots. You can do this yourself or hire someone to do it for you. If you hire someone to show or sell lots for you, be sure you conform to the laws governing the sale of real estate in your state. It is generally legal for the owner to sell on any basis.

MAKE IT EASY FOR THE BUYER

The above items are designed to make things as simple and easy as possible for your mail order customer. This buyer must be able to complete his purchase with a minimum amount of time and trouble. Remember, the mail order customer generally orders a lot or lots sight unseen. He is nervous and anxious about doing this. The low down payment and the money back guarantee is his only assurance that he is not acting foolishly.

If you handle his order efficiently, if your subdivision is easy to find, and if the lots are as advertised, you will have a bona fide sale. The proper handling of his order coupled with a good product will also result in sales of lots to this buyer's friends and relatives.

It is, of course, very important that the person who shows lots in your subdivision be neat, clean, pleasant, and reasonably intelligent. This person represents you; your reputation is in this person's hands.

I am at present using a middle-aged housewife to show lots at one of my mail order projects. She lives in the subdivision; she doesn't sell, she just tells how much she enjoys the area and takes the buyer to his lot. This has turned out to be an inexpensive way to have someone available on an everyday basis.

I never pay any fees, salary, or commissions to my representatives in advance. I always pay out of actual income from the lot sale involved. If, for some reason, the buyer makes one payment and then defaults on his contract, the balance due the representative on that sale is nullified.

This method of payment assures the land dealer that he pays only for results and only pays out of actual income from the sale.

EXAMPLE OF METHOD OF PAYING
REPRESENTATIVE

Lots sold total	$600
Monthly payment	20
Total fee due representative	60

Representative will be paid $10 from each monthly payment until he has been paid $60. In this example the representative will receive $10 per month for six months. If the buyer stops making payments after three months, then the payments to the representative stop.

In such case the representative would have received $30, the land dealer would have received $30, and the lot would go back into inventory and can be sold to someone else. If you envision the sale of many lots, you can see that your representative can build up quite a monthly income on this basis.

BUYER CONFIDENCE, KEY TO SALES

To sell land by mail, you must first have a salable product, then you must make it easy for the prospect to make the initial purchase. Next you must make it easy for him to locate and see his property. You must tailor your entire operation to assure the buyer he is doing the right thing. The key to selling land by mail is to do everything in a pleasant yet business-like manner. You must gain and keep the buyer's confidence.

READY, GO

If you have completed the purchase of your mail order land, if you have prepared and subdivided a part of this land, if you have followed the procedures outlined to this point in this chapter, then you are ready to start the actual mail order selling sequence.

To start this sequence you will need the following:

LETTERS, FORMS, AND COLLATERAL MATERIAL

Before you run one ad, before you make any effort to sell any lots by mail, do the following. Prepare all the collateral material that will be required to efficiently fill the orders that will result from your advertising.

YOU WILL NEED THE FOLLOWING ITEMS

1. Contract Form. (See Exhibit 9-7.)
2. Printed Restriction Forms. (See Exhibit 14-2.)
3. Letter of Welcome that acknowledges the order, and explains procedure. (See Exhibit 14-3.)
4. Plat Map, so buyer can pinpoint the location of the lot or lots he is buying. This map also shows proximity of lots to facilities, water and roads. (See Exhibit 14-1.)
5. Direction Map; a clear, easy to follow map, designed so the customer can drive from his home to his lot with a minimum of problems. (See Exhibit 14-4.)
6. Payment record card; designed to keep an accurate record of the financial aspects of each lot or group of lots that you sell on terms. (See Exhibit 14-5.)
7. An option collateral item is the "Guaranteed Exchange Privilege" coupon form. This is a help in creating future sales of higher priced lots. (See Exhibit 14-6.)

You may devise other items that you feel will do a better, more effective job. I suggest that you wait until your experience determines any such changes or additions.

Building Limitations and Restrictions: K. C. Colony of the Ozarks

KNOW ALL MEN BY THESE PRESENTS, that as. a part of the consideration for the conveyance of lots in KIRK C. Colony, Lake of the Ozarks, Missouri and in furtherance of
maintaining said community as a high quality location, the Parties of the Second Part
agree to the following restrictions:

1.   The described premises may be used for residence purposes only and no business
establishments of any character shall be permitted.

2.   No unsightly rubbish or litter or sign boards shall be permitted upon said premises.

3.   No structure of any kind or any addition thereto, or alteration thereof, or drive
way, fence, or wall shall be erected, placed or suffered to remain on any lot in K. C.
Colony until and unless the external design, dimension, material, color scheme, location on the lot and appurtenant slopes and grades thereof and elevation have first been
approved in writing by KIRK C. Colony. In the event KIRK C. Colony shall fail to
approve or disapprove any such requests in writing within a period of 30 days after
submission, such failure shall be considered a waiver of this requirement.

4.   No part of such structures, including porches or other extensions thereof shall be
erected closer than 40 feet to the front of the lot line, not closer than 20 feet to the
side line of any lot if such lot side line borders upon a street, otherwise, not closer
than 5 feet to any side line of any lot, except that upon written application to KIRK C.
Colony, such restrictions may be modified if the topography and terrain of any lot is
such that enforcement would work a hardship upon the owner thereof.

5.   No fence or wall of any kind shall be erected, placed or suffered to remain upon
any lot which shall extend beyond the building lines as set forth in paragraph 4 above.

6.   Septic tanks shall be built in accordance with the regulations provided by the
Department of Health of Benton County, Missouri.

7.   A permanent easement is hereby reserved along, over and under 10 feet of the
rear lot line of each lot for the purpose of providing access and use by public utilities,
drainage lines, sewers, etc.

Signed _____
                    Buyer

_____
                    Wife

Courtesy of Kirk C. Colony of Ozarks, Inc., Kansas City, Missouri

Exhibit 14-2. Printed Restriction Form

WELCOME TO THE LAKE!

You have just purchased a beautiful piece of lake property. We are sure this will result in years of pleasure for you.

We are enclosing with this letter the following items:

1. Plat map showing location of your lot (s). Please understand that these lots were surveyed and staked some time ago; some stakes may be missing or hard to find. Use size in feet of lots to measure to find your lot or lots. We advise you to take some form of measuring tape with you. Special Note: You may exchange your lot (s) for any other available lot, or lots - write for details if interested.

2. Map showing how to get to the sub-division.

3. Three (3) copies of the Land Contract Agreement to purchase Real Estate. Please sign all three copies and return them to K.C. Colony, Inc., 7511 Ozark Road, Kansas City, Missouri 64129. We will sign them and return a copy to you. These signed contracts must be returned to us within two weeks or your lots will be reallocated to another buyer. (This is because we only have a limited number of these lots available) Remember, you have a 30 day unconditional money back guarantee from the date shown on your contract.

4. Three copies (3) of Restrictions. Please read carefully and sign all copies and return them with your contract.

When we have received the three signed copies of the contract and the three signed copies of the restrictions, we will countersign the contract and return one copy of the contract and one copy of the restrictions to you. When you receive the signed copy of the contract, you may take possession of your property which includes the use of the lakefront access areas.

An accurate record of your payments will be maintained in our office. You may pay $1.00 per week per lot or $5.00 per month per lot which ever is convenient. When making payments include full name plus Lot and Block number. Writing this information on your check is a good record. Contracts can be prepaid in part or in full at anytime. After you have completed your payments you will within 60 days be furnished title by Warranty Deed to your property.

Please note: Because of the low price and easy terms we cannot afford to have any salesmen. You will need to go to the sub-division, find your property and if you have problems write us and we will help you. You get the benefit of buying property at the lowest price and easiest terms. We save the cost of salesmen and sales commissions.

Again Welcome to the Lake - enjoy your property, use the access areas - have fun.

Jack Kirk

John E. (Jack) Kirk

P.S. This sub-division has a fine lot owners association with very low annual dues. It is not mandatory that you join the association, however, they maintain the roads and the access areas plus they have many fine social programs. You will hear from one of the associations's officers and can learn more about their activities. JEK

Courtesy of Kirk C. Colony of Ozarks, Inc., Kansas City, Missouri

Exhibit 14-3. Letter of Welcome

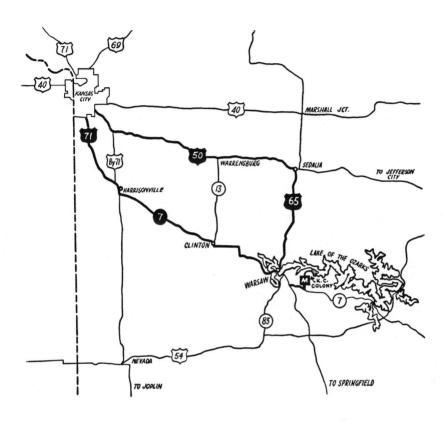

Courtesy of Kirk C. Colony of Ozarks, Inc., Kansas City, Missouri

Exhibit 14-4. Direction Map

THE CUSTOMER IS IMPATIENT

Keep in mind that your mail order customer is eager to have his order filled. As soon as the customer decides to buy, he wants action. You should always fill your mail orders as soon as your time will permit. If you have the material ready, you will be able to fill the orders with a minimum spread of time from receipt of

TRACT	BLOCK	LOTS	NAME ADDRESS			
CONTRACT DATE		DATE 1ST PMT.		AMT. PMT.		COMM.
DATE	PAYMENTS	TOTAL PMTS.	TOT. PRICE	REMARKS		BALANCE

Courtesy of Kirk C. Colony of Ozarks, Inc., Kansas City, Missouri

Exhibit 14-5. Payment Record Card

the order to its being back in the mail, on its way to your customer.

BE ACCURATE

Above all, be accurate; it is only too easy to sell the same lot twice, or not credit a payment to the customer's account. Keep a master plat map, with sold lots clearly marked. As you allocate lots to buyers, do not delay in bringing your master plat map up to date. If a customer changes his mind, defaults on payments, trades lots, etc., correct your master plat at once. Do not procrastinate in regard to the financial or lot records. Keep them accurate and current.

You have a good product, ready to sell at the right price; you have prepared the proper forms; now you are ready to advertise and sell your land by mail.

Courtesy of Kirk C. Colony of Ozarks, Inc., Kansas City, Missouri

Exhibit 14-6. Guaranteed Exchange Privilege Coupon

PROVEN ADS THAT WILL PUT
MONEY IN YOUR MAILBOX

The following pages will contain direct mail advertising that have proven sales records. These are tested ads; they have and are selling land by mail. If used properly these ads will sell land for you. You will want to adapt these ads to your specific offering. In most cases the style of these ads should be maintained. The actual sales copy should be tailored to your property, your offering, and your area.

AD NUMBER ONE IS THE HOTTEST

Ad number one (See Exhibit 14-7) is a cash with order coupon ad. It has been used by the author for over ten years. It has never failed to produce a profitable return.

CAUTION

A word of caution: like all advertising, it can be used only so many times in a given publication in a given period of time. You

EARLY BIRD SPECIAL
Your Own Lot On the
LAKE OF
THE OZARKS
$1 00
DOWN
$1 00
A WEEK

TOTAL SPECIAL PRICE
ONLY $199 00

NO INTEREST OR
OTHER CHARGES

This is a ONCE IN A LIFETIME OFFER and is in restricted PALO DURO subdivision, which is part of a 500-acre MASTER RESORT DEVELOPMENT.

All lots are full size, averaging 5,000 sq. ft. and all located within a few hundred feet of a boat dock and beach area dedicated to the perpetual use of the lot owners. This resort has a perfect location, only 123 miles from Kansas City on State maintained all weather lake road "M". Driving time from K. C. to your lot about 2½ hours. Here you will find one of the most beautiful areas on the entire lake, finest fishing, swimming, boating and just plain relaxing, plus deer, duck, quail, pheasant and rabbit hunting. Lot owners are eligible for FREE membership in the New COLONY CLUB. NOW ANYONE CAN AFFORD A PLACE ON THE LAKE, A SOUND INVESTMENT IN PLEASURE AND A HEDGE AGAINST INFLATION! Send your dollar now and tomorrow you can tell your friends about your place on the lake of the Ozarks.

ACT NOW! THIS OFFER LIMITED!

K. C. Colony, Inc.   LO
Merchandise Mart Bldg.
2201 Grand Ave., K. C. 8, Mo.

Please reserve (   ) lots. I enclose $1.00 for each lot. You will send me map showing location of my lot(s) along with purchase agreement contract for the balance of the low price of $199.00 to be paid at only $1.00 per week per lot.

NAME_____

ADDRESS_____

CITY_____STATE_____

Courtesy of Kirk C. Colony of Ozarks, Inc., Kansas City, Missouri

Exhibit 14-7. Cash with Order Coupon Ad

can, as the old story recounts, "go to the well once too often." A continuous check of results from an ad tells you when you should stop running that specific ad. Later on you can use the same ad again.

TIME OF YEAR A FACTOR

This ad can generally be used each weekend for three or four weeks. It can be repeated three times per year. I prefer mid-winter, spring and middle fall as the time of year to get best results. This is based on a mid-western climate. A different climate and area would create a different time of year factor. Testing is the only way to determine best time in your area. Timing is part of the profit principle of this ad.

LET'S LOOK AT THIS AD

Now let's examine this ad in detail. Here is an ad designed to exert maximum advertising results per dollar of cost. This is a strong, compact, wordy ad. This ad compels action and also tells a complete sales story.

WHAT, WHERE, HOW AND HOW MUCH

Starting with its strong at-a-glance heading, the prospect learns What, Where, How and How Much all in strong, bold, easy to read type.

Then the body copy tells and sells, punching out such information as maybe your only chance, fine lake property, size, location, beauty, plus other wonderful privileges, such as ease of getting to the property. Then the benefits of the pleasure aspect plus a solid hint at a potential profit.

EVERYONE BRAGS A LITTLE

The clincher is the opportunity for your customer to tell his friends that he is a landowner—that he can afford his own property on a lake.

COUPON MAKES IT EASY

Now a simple, clear-cut coupon makes it easy to order one or more of these wonderful lots.

MONEY BACK GUARANTEE

Last and maybe most important of all is the money back guarantee that assures the buyer that he can't lose. This is the confidence builder that completes this near perfect mail order ad.

STUDY DETAIL OF THIS AD

Seldom will you see or read more action-packed selling in such a small display ad. Study this ad and use it for a guide.

AD NUMBER TWO, THE QUALITY AD

Here is the same basic ad as ad number one. There is, however, one important difference. Ad number two (See Exhibit 14-8) is designed to sell lots in a higher price bracket. The use of the illustration, the larger size of the ad, the more sophisticated layout—these things all say quality. This ad, in both appearance and text, says here is your chance to own quality property at a reasonable price and on reasonable terms.

MAIN POINTS OF AD NUMBER TWO

Checking the main points of this ad results in determining the following facts.
   1. The use of a symbolic illustration rather than a photograph. This illustration gives the feel of the development and indicates the general characteristics. Be careful not to oversell or misrepresent. If the mail order customer is disappointed with the actual property because your ad overpraised or exaggerated the quality, you have not only lost a customer, you have damaged your reputation.

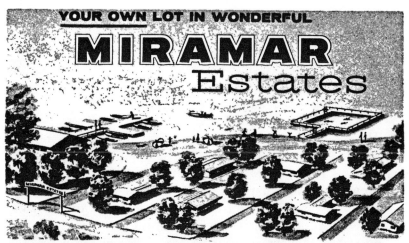

YOUR OWN LOT IN WONDERFUL
MIRAMAR Estates

LOCATED Only 123 Miles From Kansas City
On The GARDEN SPOT OF THE BEAUTIFUL
LAKE OF THE OZARKS

NOW Your Own Lot in This Wonderful Lakefront Community.

ONLY $1.00 DOWN $10.00 MONTH

TOTAL SPECIAL PRICE ONLY $399.00 NO INTEREST OR OTHER CHARGES

Absolute 30-Day Money Back Guarantee

Decide NOW to own a lot in MIRAMAR ESTATES. You are assured of being in a really fine development with restrictions that protect every lot owner. You will own property with ever increasing value, and you will enjoy a wonderful life. You can fish—boat—swim or hunt, you can have a picnic, lie on the beach, visit your own private lot owner's Club. You can have a sandwich and a coke at the Club Snack Bar. You can watch the fishermen come in with their stringers full. Why not join those happy fishermen and fill your stringer with Bass, Crappie and other varieties of fish from the waters surrounding MIRAMAR ESTATES.

Sunrise and sunset must be seen in this garden spot to be appreciated. The wonders of nature here abound, yet all the comforts of modern living are at your command. Electricity, water, telephones are readily available.

You will never have another opportunity to purchase a lot of this quality in an area of this beauty, and at the same time, to be part of such a wonderful resort development. Docks, picnic grounds, bar-b-que ovens; swimming and beach area are all dedicated to the perpetual use of the lot owners of MIRAMAR ESTATES.

ACT NOW — TOMORROW YOU CAN TELL YOUR FRIENDS ABOUT YOUR LOT IN WONDERFUL MIRAMAR ESTATES.

LOCATED ON NEW ALL WEATHER STATE ROAD "M".

TV2 MAIL THIS COUPON TODAY
YOU PAY ONLY $399.00
NOTHING MORE! MIRAMAR ESTATES lots are sold INTEREST FREE with NO HIDDEN CHARGES! Title is by Warranty Deed and a Title Policy is optional.
Prices will be increased soon
ACT AT ONCE.
30 Day Money Back Guarantee

MIRAMAR ESTATES/Merchandise Mart Bldg. • 2201 Grand Ave., K. C. 8, Mo.
Please reserve ( ) lots. I enclose $1.00 for each lot. You will send me map showing location of my lot(s) along with full information and purchase agreement contract for the balance of the low price of $399.00 to be paid at only $10.00 per month per lot.

NAME _____

ADDRESS_____

CITY_____STATE_____

Courtesy of Kirk C. Colony of Ozarks, Inc., Kansas City, Missouri

Exhibit 14-8. Quality Ad

2. The headline copy, "Your Own Lot in Wonderful Miramar Estates," combined with the illustration establishes the What, the Where, and says quality. The ad then repeats Where and What.

3. Now price and terms to complete our attention-getting method of saying, *what, where,* and *how much.* Note: Truth in Lending Laws may require details of interest rate, etc. Check with your lawyer for latest rulings.

4. The body copy says here is your opportunity to own property in a really fine resort development. This copy explains the pleasures and the joys that await the buyer of property in Miramar Estates. Again you find the line that says you can tell your friends about your lot on the lake. Here you offer immediate enjoyment to the buyer. He doesn't even have to wait to see or use his property. His pleasure begins with the telling of his purchase.

5. Next, of course, is the effective coupon. The coupon says it's easy to buy; just indicate how many lots, fill in name and address, send the token down payment, and you own lake property. This action coupon has proven to have a tremendous sales appeal.

6. Ad number two also guarantees satisfaction.

BOTH ADS ONE AND TWO ARE PROVEN SALES PRODUCERS

Ads one and two are both examples of mail order advertising that will, if tailored to the land being offered, bring in results. Again, let it be clear that the product must be worthy of the advertising. You are a reputable dealer in land—promise only that which you can and will deliver. In direct mail selling, honesty is as necessary as having a product to sell.

FILL THE ORDERS

You have studied two basic ads that can be used to put money in your mailbox. Along with that money will be orders for your land. Using the collateral material outlined in this chapter, we will follow step by step the procedure used to fill the orders you receive.

PROCEDURE

Here is the procedure for filling orders as they arrive in your mail.

1. Arrange your collateral material to be available in proper sequence.
2. Mark on your large plat map those lots you will use to fill orders in this price range. (I use colors to show allocated, sold and unsold lots.) These lots will for ad number one be your lowest priced usable lots. In all subdivisions there will be some lots that are very sub-standard: do not use these to fill mail orders.
3. Opening the first envelope we find it contains a short letter, a check, and a filled-in coupon ordering two lots. The letter requests that the two lots be located side by side. The coupon has the buyer's name and address carefully printed. The check is in the amount of the token down payment for two lots.
4. Using three copies of the contract for deed form, you will fill in the blanks as follows: The date, the buyer's full name, his complete address, his phone number if available, then the name of the subdivision lot numbers, block number, and tract number. If a maintenance or other annual fee is charged, show the amount per lot. Then show the total purchase price, interest charge, total time balance, down payment credited, the total time balance after deduction of the down payment, the number of monthly payments, the amount of the monthly payment and the beginning payment date. Now mark an "X" on each copy, showing where the buyer is to sign. Check Truth in Lending law for exact copy now required for interest charges.
5. Take three copies of the restrictions and mark an "X" on each copy to show where the buyer is to sign.
6. Now take the plat map and mark the location of the two lots you are allocating to this buyer. As you do this, also mark the same two lots on your large master plat map. You can indicate last name of buyer as an added record on the large map. Do this on the large map in pencil; in case the buyer doesn't complete his purchase, you can erase the mark and name and allocate these lots to another buyer.
7. Now carefully address a suitable envelope and insert the following items:
   A. Three copies of the Contract for Deed

B. Three copies of the Restrictions
C. One copy of Welcome and Instruction letter
D. One copy of Plat Map
E. One copy of Direction Map
F. One copy of Exchange Coupon

Be sure to put adequate postage on the envelope before you mail it.

THE SECOND LETTER

We open the second letter and find it is from a person whose order had been filled a week before. This letter contains the three copies of the Contract for Deed, each signed by the buyer, and also enclosed are three copies of the restrictions, which are also signed. You now sign and date the three copies of the Contract for Deed. With your signature, the contract is now in full force.

Now make out a payment card. Be sure to show all details. These payment cards are kept in alphabetical order in a file box. I also use a cross file by lot and block numbers. Using this cross file system, it is possible to check on each lot and lot buyer using either the name of buyer or only the lot and block number. Use full names, including middle name or initial. You will be amazed how many people have the same first and last name.

You now return one copy of Contract for Deed and one copy of Restrictions to buyer. You keep one copy of each at your home, and keep the third copy of each in your safety deposit box at your bank. These contracts are valuable—treat them like money, because that is what they are.

OPEN YOUR MAIL, TAKE OUT MONEY

You have now followed one of the procedures for selling land by mail. You are tasting for the first time the pleasure of opening your mail and finding it full of money. It is easy, it is a pleasure, and you can do it, if you follow the method.

MAIL ORDER SALES FROM INQUIRIES

Another method of selling land by mail is the use of inquiry-producing advertising. These inquiry-type ads will in most cases be small, and will be placed in the classified section of newspapers. Here is a sample inquiry-type ad that proved very effective.

LOT ON TABLE ROCK LAKE
FULL PRICE ONLY $299.00 — $5.00 DOWN
$10.00 MONTH — WRITE MR. SMITH
ADDRESS

This ad not only generated a considerable number of sale-producing inquiries, it also made actual by mail sales. People actually sent $5.00 along with their inquiry and ask that a lot be reserved for them.

The most amazing fact about this ad is its low cost. Depending on the circulation of the newspaper this ad will cost as little as $2.00 and no more than $20.00 per insertion.

Here is proof that it doesn't take large amounts of money to test and sell land by mail.

If you will study this ad you will discover the secret of its success. It was a combination of the product, the price and the terms. The opportunity to own any piece of resort property for only $299.00 and terms of only $5.00 down $10.00 per month is almost irresistable. The right product, at the right price and on the right terms—this is indeed the magic combination. Whether you are buying or selling, this is the combination that gets the job done.

TWO WORDS CHANGE A BAD
AD TO A GOOD ONE

Now take a look at an inquiry ad that failed. This ad did not pull one inquiry and did not make one sale. The ad appeared in the same newspaper as the successful ad and cost more money because it had more words and required more space.

Here is the ad that failed.

LAKE FRONT LOTS
TABLE ROCK LAKE
THE FINEST—NOT CHEAP
PHONE, WRITE OR VISIT

MR. SMITH
ADDRESS
PHONE

Not one inquiry, not one sale. What is wrong with this ad? It was the author's opinion that the statement "NOT CHEAP" was the culprit. It seems that most people want to feel that they are buying at a low price in relation to the value of the product.

Here is the same ad with only two words changed. Read this revised ad and compare it to the non-producing ad.

LAKE FRONT LOTS
TABLE ROCK LAKE
THE FINEST—BARGAIN PRICES
PHONE, WRITE OR VISIT
MR. SMITH
ADDRESS
PHONE

This ad brought in inquiries and produced sales. Replacing the "Not Cheap" copy with "Bargain Prices" put the sell in this ad. (Note: The change from "Not Cheap" to "Bargain Prices" is based on the prices of the lots being in the higher price bracket yet being a bargain on a comparative basis. Both ads tell the truth.) These two ads prove that the test of an ad is always based on the results obtained for the dollar expended. In the chapter on advertising, you will learn how to put the selling words in all types of advertising.

After you have developed the ads that will bring in inquiries, you must convert these inquiries into sales. Here is the method that does that job for you.

Prepare a letter similar to the following.

Dear Mr. Blank:

Thank you for your request for information about lots on Table Rock Lake. These are full size lots and each one is a beautiful building site. They are located in one of the finest subdivisions on the lake.

Enclosed with this letter are the following items.

1. PLAT MAP with descriptive information about the subdivision. *Note* that the lots available for $299.00 are clearly indicated.

    2. DIRECTION MAP to make it easy for you to drive to the property.

    3. LOT RESERVATION FORM, so if you can't come to the lake at this time you can reserve a lot or lots.

If you can come to the lake now, you will have an enjoyable trip. You might take the time to do a little boating and fishing—all on a trip to examine the wonderful lots that are available.

If you can't come to the lake at this time, please use the enclosed reservation form. You can reserve a lot or lots by merely sending a $5.00 deposit (refundable) for each lot you want. We will select the best lot available and will send you a Contract for Deed showing your balance to be paid at only $10.00 per month per lot. Interest is only 6 percent.

These lots are sold on our 90 day inspection arrangement. Your order is not accepted until you have examined the property. If at the time of your personal examination you are not completely satisfied, your deposit is refunded.

Act now; as you can see by the enclosed plat map, there are only a limited number of these lots available.

Again, thank you for your interest. I will be looking forward to seeing you at the lake.

                                     Cordially,

The signature on this letter can be yours or the person you have handling sales on the property.

You will, of course, tailor all material to your specific land and your specific offering. This material can be surprisingly effective in creating sales.

PUTTING THE FINAL TOUCH ON THE SALE

Next, you must have some arrangement for the buyers and prospective buyers to see the property. The same method is used here as outlined in the section on selling lots by mail using the coupon ad. This will give you the method you can use to complete the sales initiated by mail inquiries.

UPGRADE TO MORE PROFITS

Whether the initial sale is made using the coupon ad or the inquiry ad, the results will generally be the sale of one or more of your lowest priced lots. The sale of a low-priced lot to a new customer can start a chain reaction. This reaction can lead to sales of your more expensive lots, and to sales of many lots to friends and relatives of the initial buyer. This chain reaction will in many cases happen naturally. It can, however, be accelerated by the action taken by the land seller. Here are the methods and materials that will upgrade and increase your sales volume and your profits.

First we must show our low price lot owner how easy it is for him to own a better lot or lots. We can accomplish this in a number of ways.

SELF-UPGRADING SUBDIVISION

If you have your available lots clearly marked as to price and terms you have a self-upgrading subdivision. Each mail order lot customer can easily compare his lots to other lots available in the subdivision.

As your low price lot owner becomes familiar with the area, he can see that for only a few dollars more per month he can own a better lot or more lots, or lots closer to or fronting on the water. He can sell himself, and you reap the profits from a larger dollar sale with no sales or advertising costs.

I use the guaranteed trade-in form to accelerate this upgrade selling. The buyer knows that he will receive the full amount he has paid for his present lots if he trades for more lots or for better lots. This guaranteed trade in form actually acts as a selling tool. It brings to the lot owner's mind the fact that he can trade up to better lots. This is your action creating a reaction, and this reaction making you more profit.

If you mark your lots clearly and with proper information, they will be self-selling. If you give each buyer a guaranteed exchange coupon, this will create sales action. This is how you can establish your own self-service subdivision.

DIRECT MAIL UPGRADES

Once your subdivision is in operation, once you have lot owners, you can start to upgrade by mail. Your present lot owners have already shown that your area meets their requirements. Now you have a pre-sold prospect for that better, higher priced lot.

All you need to do is to show these prospects how easy it is for them to own more lots or better lots. Here you make everything as simple as possible.

SIMPLE FACTS MAKE BIG PROFITS

To sell by direct mail, you must have something to mail to the prospect. You have a choice: folders, flyers, or a letter. You may decide to use more than one of these items at the same time. In the next chapter you will be given tips on how to write the copy for this type of advertising and sales promotion material. For now we will only show examples and examine the methods used to motivate the prospect.

Present your facts to the prospect in a simple, easy to understand way. Tell and Sell is not just a cute sounding play on words, it is a fact. A flyer is a simple, single sheet advertising piece. (See Exhibit 14-9.) It is different from a letter in that it generally uses art and/or special lettering. A folder as its name implies, is a folded piece of printed advertising literature. (See Exhibit 14-10.) A folder is generally printed on a good grade of paper, with art and special type; it may be printed in more than one color.

A well-written letter is a very strong direct mail sales tool. Keep these letters simple, direct, and above all, believable. Tell and explain the advantages of your offering. Make it easy for the prospect to understand what and how.

The use of an order form is one way to make it easy. If the prospect can simply fill out the form and attach his check, the prospect can and will act while the impulse to buy is strong. If, however, he can't quite figure out how to complete the deal, he may delay doing anything. This delay can and will cost you many sales.

SIMPLE + EASY = SALES

Make it easy—Make it simple—Help the prospect become a customer. Help the customer buy more and better lots. This is the

TABLE ROCK LAKE

STONE COUNTY

SHELL KNOB—VIOLA, MISSOURI

HIGHWAY 39

- Choice Building Sites
- Wide Blacktop Streets
- Water System
- Electricity
- Butane
- Telephones
- Maintenance

Beauty that belongs to you. A gracious life in a setting of natural wonders.

PRIVATE • PROTECTED • MAINTAINED

"AN ENTIRE PRIVATE PENINSULA"

SCANDIA

SCANDIA

"FOR THE FEW"

An entire private peninsula located on beautiful Table Rock Lake . . . this development contains a limited number of lakefront and lakeview building sites . . . controlled access to the entire property . . . secluded yet near to gourmet restaurant, shopping center and a host of recreation facilities.

NEVER A CROWD . . . NOT OPEN TO THE PUBLIC

YOUR OWN PRIVATE SHANGRI-LA

THIS IS BEAUTY THAT WILL BE SHARED BY ONLY A FORTUNATE FEW.

PRIVATE ROAD

PRIVATE ROAD

Courtesy of Kirk C. Colony of Ozarks, Inc., Kansas City, Missouri

Exhibit 14-9. Direct Mail Flyer

LOCATED Only **123 Miles** From Kansas City
On The **GARDEN SPOT OF THE BEAUTIFUL**

LAKE ᴼᶠ THE OZARKS

NOW Your Own Lot in This Wonderful Lakefront Community.

Decide NOW to own a lot in MIRAMAR ESTATES. You are assured of being in a really fine development with restrictions that protect every lot owner. You will own property with ever increasing value, and you will enjoy a wonderful life. You can fish—boat—swim or hunt, you can have a picnic, lie on the beach. You can have a sandwich and a coke at the Club Snack Bar. You can watch the fishermen come in with their stringers full. Why not join those happy fishermen and fill your stringer with Bass, Crappie and other varieties of fish from the waters surrounding MIRAMAR ESTATES.

Sunrise and sunset must be seen in this garden spot to be appreciated. The wonders of nature here abound, yet all the comforts of modern living are at your command. Electricity, water, telephones are readily available.
You will never have another opportunity to purchase a lot of this quality in an area of this beauty, and at the same time, to be part of such a wonderful resort development. Docks, picnic grounds, bar-b-que ovens; swimming and beach area are all dedicated to the perpetual use of the lot owners of MIRAMAR ESTATES.
ACT NOW—TOMORROW YOU CAN TELL YOUR FRIENDS ABOUT YOUR LOT IN WONDERFUL MIRAMAR ESTATES.

YOUR OWN LOT IN WONDERFUL

MIRAMAR
Estates

LARGE ESTATE SIZE LOTS 5000 SQ. FT.

Courtesy of Kirk C. Colony of Ozarks, Inc., Kansas City, Missouri

Exhibit 14-10. Direct Mail Folder

way to increase volume, decrease sales and advertising costs. This means more dollars of profits in your pocket.

FRIENDS AND RELATIVES

Ninety-nine percent of the readers of this book have never heard of Braymer, Missouri. As a point of interest, I will explain that it is an attractive, very small rural community (population 874).

In one of my resort subdivisions located about 150 miles from Braymer, we have an area of lots that is now known as Braymerville. The reason this area has acquired the name Braymerville is an important lesson in resort lot selling. In this area you can see graphically how friends and relatives can pyramid lot sales.

One man who lives in Braymer, Missouri, bought a lot in this subdivision. He liked the area, he was happy with his purchase, and he told his friends and relatives. One of these bought the lot next to the first lot owner. During the next twelve months over twenty lots were sold in this specific area to persons living in or near Braymer, Missouri. At this date, there are many attractive cottages and lake homes in the area now referred to as Braymerville.

All of these lot sales were made without any advertising. These sales were made by mail to friends and relatives of lot owners. As each new prospect became a lot owner he was shown how he could be a salesman for lots in the Braymerville area of this subdivision.

The natural desire of these people of common interest to be together was assisted by letters telling them how they could help their friends and relatives enjoy this lake resort area.

NATURAL ACTION WITH A LITTLE SHOVE

Natural action in this example would have sold many lots. This natural action was given a shove, and it resulted in the sale of more lots than if the shove were missing. Don't depend on natural action alone. Accept gratefully the benefits from such action. Then put that extra shove, that extra push, for that is the action you can depend on.

Don't forget that the really successful person is the action person. The extra sales, the extra profits, come from that action. Your customer can be your best salesman if he is motivated. Direct mail to these customers can be the factor that motivates.

YOUR PERSONAL MAIL ORDER FORTUNE

Don't let anyone tell you that you cannot make money selling by mail. Don't let anyone tell you not to deal in land by mail. Conform to the proper laws and regulations. Have a good product. Sell that product in an honest, straightforward manner. Study the method, plan, and test. Then you will be able to put the results in your bank account. As sure as you follow the Method, as sure as you put forth the effort, you will make money from dealing in land.

You may make a fortune.

SHORT SUCCESS STORIES

The Ad That Costs Nothing

The dollar-down ad (See Exhibit 14-7) appeared in TV Guide magazine. It brought in 162 lot orders; $1.00 was enclosed for each lot ordered. Ad cost $149; income from down payments, $162. Land sales resulting from this ad here in excess of $15,000.

Here is advertising that is self-liquidating. This is admittedly an exception. It is an example of advertising the right offer, on the right terms at the right time, and selecting the right method of presenting this to the public.

The Ad That Seemed to Fail!

The same ad appeared in the sports section of a small town newspaper. This ad resulted in only one order, one dollar down payment and the sale of $199 worth of land. It was a failure, or was it?

The man who bought that one lot from that ad had friends and relatives. His friends and relatives had friends and relatives.

At last count, fourteen lots sold for over $4,000 as a result of the ad, the man, and his friends and relatives. The story does not end here—more sales will result in the future. The product was good, the ad was truthful, and a happy customer did the rest. The ad that seemed to fail was really success in disguise.

Special Note regarding land sales by mail, inter-state sales and other:

The Interstate Land Sales Act of 1968, effective April 28, 1969. This Federal Land Sales Act requires registration of land developers unless meeting certain exemption requirements.

Certain states also have their own land sales laws.

If terms are offered, you must also comply with the requirements of the Truth in Lending Act.

Check with your lawyer before you subdivide or make your sales offering.

15

Advertising and Sales Promotions That Really Produce for You

To know where and how to advertise is one of the key profit principles for the dealer in land. In this chapter you will learn land advertising based on the combined experiences of a number of successful land dealers. From this, you will be able to formulate your own advertising and sales promotion plans.

Advertising is bringing information to the attention of a person or persons for the purpose of creating sales. We tell the merits of our product, we explain the benefits the buyer will receive—then we make it as easy as possible for the prospect to become a buyer and obtain these benefits.

MEDIA

The term "media" means the vehicle that will carry your advertising sales message to the public. You have a wide choice of advertising media. You can choose from newspapers, magazines, direct mail, radio, and television.

The actual decision as to which of the various media to use is not difficult. The selling of land lends itself best to certain of these media. In the majority of cases you will only use one or two of the listed media to attain your sales goal.

NEWSPAPERS

You could literally eliminate all other advertising media except newspaper and be a successful dealer in land. The newspaper, as the advertising media for selling land, is so strong that it dominates all the other media combined. This dominance does not mean that we should or will ignore the other media. It does mean we will spend the most time and effort on the subject of advertising land using newspapers as our advertising media.

WHY NEWSPAPER ADVERTISING IS BEST

Newspapers reach more prospective land buyers per dollar expended than the other media. The newspaper covers a known specific area on an almost saturation basis. In many areas there is only one newspaper. In areas where there are more than one paper, you will find that one of these dominates your market.

To reach the mass market we use the lowest cost advertising media. In general this will be the newspaper. In addition to this ability to reach the mass of prospects at low cost, we have buyer habit. The buying habits of the American consumer is heavily newspaper oriented. This buyer habit is doubly strong in regard to buying real estate. The newspapers have always been a dominant advertising tool in the buying and selling of all types of real estate property. The average person interested in buying or selling real estate will almost without exception consult newspaper advertising. Newspapers have two types of advertising that can be used by the dealer in land. These two types are display and classified advertisements.

DISPLAY ADVERTISEMENTS

Display ads are those you see spread all through the newspaper. Such ads cover every conceivable product and service. In most cases, these ads are not under a product or service listing or heading.

In many cases, certain products or services will be grouped in a specific section of the paper. An example would be auto tires and auto accessories. You will in most cases find such items are advertised in or adjacent to the sports page or sports section. This placement is based on the masculine nature of the majority of prospects for such products. Sports fans are predominantly male. Advertisements for masculine products will have a higher male readership if such ads appear in the sports section of the paper.

SELLING LAND WITH DISPLAY ADS

In selling land using display ads, the following rules on ad placement can increase the sales results.

1. Business property should be advertised in the business and financial section of the paper.
2. Resort property should be advertised in the sports, fishing hunting and in some cases the resort section of the paper.
3. City residential lots should be advertised in the section of general readership. Advertise such lots where the department stores advertise merchandise for the family and the home.
4. Country property that is being offered to city and suburban prospects should be advertised in the general readership section as defined under number three for selling city residential lots.
5. Country property for sale to country people should be in the section where agricultural news and information is reported. Small town newspapers should also be considered.

Advertising land for sale is a matter of deciding who would be most interested in your specific land. You then decide what section of the newspaper that person is most likely to read. You can request placement of your ad in a specific part of most newspapers. Such placement is generally not guaranteed. It has been the experience of the author that most newspapers will place your ad in the section you request.

PLACEMENT—THE KEY TO SALES

The following is an example of the great importance of the placement of an ad in a specific section of a newspaper. The author was placing his very first land selling ad in a newspaper. I had never sold any land by any method up to the time of this incident. I went to the display advertising department of the local newspaper. I carried with me the rough copy for what I hoped would be a good ad to sell my land. I was lucky; the man at the display advertising desk was not only an intelligent person, he also felt he should be helpful to a novice.

He and I went over my ad copy. He helped work out the parts of the ad that should be in large type. He acted as the advertising specialist and helped me achieve an attractive attention-getting ad. He then suggested that I have the ad run on the Rod & Gun page of the paper. I had never heard of the Rod & Gun page. I soon learned that most persons who have an interest in fishing, hunting, boating and other phases of outdoor life were readers of the Rod & Gun page. The reason was simple—the Rod & Gun page carried news and articles on subjects of interest to such persons.

The land I was advertising was lake property. The logical prospects for such land were the people who would read the Rod & Gun page. I followed this man's advice, and the next Sunday my ad appeared in the paper on the Rod & Gun page.

The results were amazing. I received a substantial number of orders for lots in my subdivision. This ad was the start of the profitable part of my land venture. Now a sequel to this story.

I decided that my ad might do better if I had it placed in the Resort section of the paper. I ordered the position change, and it appeared the following Sunday among a great many ads for vacation spots, resorts, motels, etc. The results—less than 20 percent as many orders for my lots. The following Sunday I put my ad back on the Rod & Gun page and my sales increased.

Many papers do not have a page called Rod & Gun, but most papers do have hunting, fishing, boating, and similar news in their sports section. It has been my experience that resort property can best be advertised in the sports section of the newspaper.

The important point in this example is, place your display ad where the most people who should be interested in your specific land are most likely to see it. This placement profit principle is of great importance in planning your advertising.

SELLING LAND WITH CLASSIFIED ADS

The newspaper is the prime, basic real estate advertising media. The classified advertising section of the newspaper is the prime section of the prime media. The sales results obtained per advertising dollar spent in classified advertising can approach the unbelievable.

It is not unknown for a five dollar classified ad to sell a half-million-dollar property. The author found and purchased his first major piece of resort property through a very small classified ad. This land was then subdivided and sold for fifty times the purchase price, and much of its resale was through the use of newspaper display and classified ads. You must understand that the buying habits of people contribute to the amazing results you can obtain by using a low-cost classified ad.

In major cities and to a lesser degree in small towns, the general public use the classified ad section as their buy and sell bible. When these people want to sell almost anything they run a classified ad in their local paper. When they want to buy something they look in the classified ad section. It is buyer habit and it works like magic.

In addition to the buyer habit on all items, classified advertising is best known as the place where all types of real property are advertised. Persons interested in buying any form of real estate will almost without exception look in the classified section of their local paper. It is so widely used that types of property and even geographical areas have separate headings to assist the prospect in locating exactly the type property in a specific area he desires. To assist you in developing the ability to write classified ads that will sell, we will analyze a typical land selling classified ad.

MERRIAM—½ Acre, C-1, perfect for restaurant, private club, sell, lease, take part ownership, name, address, phone.

The above ad appeared in a major newspaper in the classfied ad section under the listing of "Business Properties." In three lines it contained the following information.
1. Location, everyone in the readership area of the paper used knew that Merriam is a local small suburban community.
2. Size of the property.
3. Zoning
4. Suggested uses
5. Selection of methods for a person to obtain the use or ownership of the property.
6. Who to contact and how.

This ad cost less than $5.00 per insertion in a major newspaper. It gave enough information to create action from a prospect. It was placed in the classified advertising section under the heading that any intelligent prospect would use as a source for locating such property.

If the seller was not willing to lease, sell or participate, it would have been advisable to have included the price and a suggestion of terms. Because the seller was extremely flexible regarding sale or lease of the property, price became a secondary factor.

The study of the classified advertising section of any newspaper will be of great help in developing the ability to compose such ads. A word of advice: Do not consider a classified ad to be a telegram. Give all needed details; don't use abbreviations. You are dealing with a very low cost ad. A few extra words may put the sell in your ad. When you have written a classified ad, ask someone to read it. Then ask them to tell you what it says. If this reader has a clear understanding of your product and your offer, plus the knowledge of how and who to contact to take the next step toward its purchase, then your ad is complete. It is very easy to leave an important element out of a classified ad.

Let us study what information most classified ads used to sell land should contain.

1. What
2. Where
3. How much
4. How
5. Who

You should in general tell what you have for sale, where it is located, how much it costs, how it can be purchased and who it can be purchased from.

Let us examine another classified ad—this one to sell a piece of country property to an urban or suburban prospect.

CLOSE IN RANCH

6 Acres with creek in Jackson County, Missouri for only $15,500.00. Terms. 3 acres in pasture, rest wooded. Fruit and Walnut trees, 5 room house overlooking woods and creek. Commuters special at $15,500.00. Call NAME – PHONE

The what, where and how much is covered in the first sentence.

Then more sell and a perfect close that restates the fact it is so close you could commute. Finally the price is special, then the who in a name and local phone number.

The key words used to attract readership was CLOSE IN RANCH. Most urban and suburban prospects for country property want it close in. They may want to commute to their city job until they retire. The word ranch or ranchette is a kind of symbol to many people. It has a pleasant big time sound.

This ad tells all and makes it easy for the interested person to take further action. This type ad has a proven sales record. Variations of this ad can sell land for you. Study ads of this type and make sure your ads conform to the basic tell to sell profit principle.

PRACTICE AND TEST

We have said before, the good ad is the ad that creates sales. To write a good classified ad you must practice and test. Based on your studied knowledge of your product and your prospects, write your ad. Select the media and select the section where your ad will appear. Select the days or day of the week that your ad is to be published.

Place your order to have your ad appear, and check the results. If you feel the results were less than they should be, do the following. Restudy your product, your offer and your advertising. Make changes and repeat the process. If you follow this method, if you plan and then test, you will have few failures, and even the failures can be used as a guide to success.

MAGAZINE ADVERTISING

In general, you will consider magazine advertising only if you are operating on a large scale. Your product must have a much wider area appeal, as magazines normally cover larger areas.

Many magazines now sell regional advertising schedules. As an example, you can buy advertising in a national magazine that will appear in Kansas but not in California. Each magazine offering such regional advertising has its own breakdown as to what states or parts of states are covered in each regional breakdown.

Some magazines such as *TV Guide* are published on a regional basis due to the magazine's basic content. *Sunset* magazine is big in the west, but doesn't exist to an appreciable extent in the east. You must decide who is a legitimate prospect for your land. You must then consider the cost factors in relation to potential dollar sales income. You must plan your advertising with knowledge of cost relation to expected results.

SPECIAL ADVANTAGES

There are two special advantages advertisements appearing in magazines have. One is quality impression. Prospects are inclined to consider items advertised in magazines as being of higher quality than those advertised in local newspapers. Two is the lifetime of an advertisement appearing in a magazine. People read magazines for days, even weeks, after the magazine is received. Orders or inquiries will come in for weeks, even months, from such advertising. In contrast, newspaper advertising is generally instant reaction, then nothing.

HOW TO DECIDE

If you feel that your land offer is large enough and broad enough to make magazine advertising pay, if you decide to try such advertising, you should get professional help from an advertising agency. I would never recommend preparation of a magazine ad by other than a professional. I would further recommend the use of professional guidance in the selection of the specific publication. Magazine advertising is not for the do-it-yourself dealer in land. I repeat, if you decide you need magazine advertising, get yourself an advertising agency.

RADIO

When talking of radio, I am reminded of the old story of the man reported dead. His retort was that the reports of his death had been greatly exaggerated. The reports of the decline and death of radio due to a sickness called TV have also been greatly exaggerated.

Radio is a healthy, growing mass audience entertainment and advertising media. If is unfortunately not as effective in selling land as it is in selling other products.

The author has experimented and tested radio advertising to sell country and resort property. The results have been very poor. I cannot, therefore, recommend radio to you, the dealer in land. I would not, however, want you to close your mind to radio as an advertising media. The future can bring about many changes. Radio may become a suitable advertising media at some point in time. You should remain flexible and receptive to all possible changes.

TELEVISION

If magazine advertising is for the big area dealer, then television is for the big local dealer. Keep in mind, however, that television advertising is EXPENSIVE.

In dealing in television, because of its costs and the need for the production of a TV tape or film, use an advertising man or agency. Select one that has experience in producing television commercials. Count your money very carefully when you contemplate television advertising. It can sell land for you. Unfortunately, it has also contributed to the bankruptcy of some business firms. I repeat, television advertising is EXPENSIVE—approach with caution.

LETTERS, FLYERS, BROCHURES, MAPS, ETC.

The simplest form of advertising is a sales letter. Sales letters are inexpensive to prepare, and if written properly can produce sales at a very low cost. The basic rules for a sales letter are as follows:

1. Present the facts in easy to understand language. Do not be fancy in your choice of words.
2. Tell and sell: here you present the facts in an interesting and sales-oriented manner.

3. Be sure you have considered the desires of the prospect in relation to your product.
4. Last, and very important, tell them how to take the action that converts them from prospect to buyer.

FLYERS

A flyer is in reality a sales letter that has been embellished with special type and in certain cases with illustrations or photos. A flyer is generally printed on a colored paper. It looks like an advertising piece; it is not as personal as a letter. It is difficult to decide when the use of a flyer is better than the use of a letter.

The author has a leaning toward the use of a letter. I have, however, used a flyer when I felt the use of photos or art would make my offer come through to the prospect with more sales impact.

BROCHURES

A brochure is an elaborate multi-color folder to advertise your land offering. Brochures are widely used to sell land for use as permanent or vacation building sites for individuals. Here you can use color, photos, maps and lettering to create an advertising piece that creates desire. If your prospect desires your product, he will in most cases find a way to buy that product.

Your sales job is to find the prospect, create the desire, and then complete the sale. A well-written, well-prepared brochure will do the job.

A brochure is not difficult to conceive; however, it can be difficult for a person who does not have advertising training to produce. I would suggest that here again you consider obtaining help from a professional advertising man or an advertising agency.

MAPS—SUBDIVISION AND DIRECTIONAL

The use of subdivision plat maps is necessary from a practical standpoint. These are the maps that pinpoint the location of specific lots or tracts of land. These are the maps that show the shape and size of the property you have sold or are selling. In addition, such a map can show the buyer the relationship of his property to roads, access and recreational areas, etc.

An equally important use of the subdivision plat map is as a sales tool. Note that our MIRAMAR brochure is also a plat map. It shows each lot and each lot's relationship to the water and to the access areas. A customer could select a lot without ever seeing the land. He would only need to have the terrain of his lot described to complete his picture of his land.

A strong sales message tells and sells the area and the facilities. The plat map shows, tells and sells. See Exhibit 14-10 for Miramar Estates. Read the copy; look at the map. This is an example of a complete self-selling plat map. It has a sales record that is hard to believe. In simple terms, it's a sales tool that gets the job done.

The best way to understand how to prepare and use these advertising sales tools is to study the samples, read the examples, and consult with professional advertising people. Then plan and test. As I have said before, the only true test of any of your advertising is the results per dollar of cost. Keep records; measure the inquiries and sales resulting from each sales tool. Compute these results based on the cost factor of each. Repeat the successful; learn from the failures. Keep in mind that tastes and desires change. Be sure your advertising and sales methods keep up with the times.

FREE ADVERTISING

Up to this point we have been discussing advertising and sales promotions that cost money. There is, happily, a great area of free advertising. We will call this "word of mouth advertising." In your land dealings, this free word of mouth advertising will be at work with or without your knowledge or consent.

YOUR REPUTATION CAN ADVERTISE
GOOD OR BAD

This free advertising can be detrimental as well as helpful. If your product is good, the word is good. If your product is bad, the word is bad. There are ways to be certain that almost all of the word of mouth advertising about your project will be good. You can be sure this free advertising is working for you if you follow these five principles:

1. Deliver a good product
2. Sell that product at a fair price
3. Keep your word
4. Treat people fairly
5. Deliver what you promise

J.C. Penney, a man of great fame and fortune, founded his original store based on the golden rule. The results are known the world over.

You can be certain that you are on the road to success if you use the golden rule part of the J.C. Penney success story. Do not be led down the garden path of dishonesty. There are some people who will tell you that it takes a little dishonesty to make money. There is no such thing as a little dishonesty. You are either an honorable, honest person, or you are a dishonest person. The principle of word of mouth advertising works for the honest man and against the dishonest man. If you adhere to the five principles listed in this chapter, then word of mouth advertising will—

MAKE YOUR FORTUNE

This great big wonderful world of free advertising and sales help is just waiting to help you make your land fortune. It can and will sell land, and it will even perpetuate itself—each new buyer becomes a word of mouth advertising salesman. All of these people help you make sales, and sales are money in your pocket.

You can increase the effectiveness of these free salesmen in a number of ways. I would recommend starting with courtesy. Elmer Wheeler, the great sales teacher and writer, claims that courtesy is the greatest of all sales tools. I have personnally proven him right in many actual business ventures. To see how courtesy works, do the following. Take the time to thank a person who has said something nice about you or your product. Thank that person verbally in front of others. Watch the pleasure this person feels from your simple act of courtesy. To thank a person is very easy, yet many people do not do it.

This use of integrity and courtesy to increase your sales should be a conscious effort. It should be part of your sales and advertising plan. Put such a plan into effect with all the people around you—Your friends, relatives and business associates. They are, after all, no different from your customers. If they like you, if they feel you are an honest person, they will recommend you and your products.

A WHOLE NEW WORLD

The conscious use of the golden rule, which includes courtesy, can and will open up an entire world of people wanting to help you succeed. With all of these people selling you and your product, it will be difficult for you to fail. Harness this word of mouth free advertising to your land deals and your fortune is made.

16

Tested Fortune
Making Programs

If after reading the preceding chapters you have decided to become a dealer in land, these tested programs will act as a blueprint.

FIRST PROFIT

Finding your first opportunity to profit in land is not difficult.

Select the area.
Study real estate advertising in that area.
Advise real estate brokers of your desires.
Develop a land use plan.

ACT—BUY

When you find a good deal, buy it. Do not wait for the best deal or the perfect deal. It is a simple truth that the perfect deal does not exist. You will make your profit not in perfection, but you will profit in those properties that are good buys.

I repeat: WHEN YOU FIND A GOOD DEAL ON A DESIR-ABLE PIECE OF LAND IN THE AREA OF YOUR CHOICE—BUY IT.

ACT—SELL

Now you own a tract of land. You bought it using the methods in this book. You bought it at a fair price, with terms you can afford and on a basis that fits your land use plan.

Now use any of a number of methods outlined in this book to turn this land investment into a land profit. Pick the method that fits your area, your land, and your own land use plan. Keep in mind that you did not buy this land to keep. You are going to make your fortune dealing in land. To make that fortune you must deal and deal again.

You merely apply the methods for dividing, improving, advertising and selling part or all of this, your first tract of land.

Study, plan, then start your sales program. Test and retest as necessary. If you follow the steps as outlined, your first land investment will now be your first land profit.

COUNT YOUR PROFITS

The profits from this, your first deal in land, will not only be in money. This is the deal where you also profit from learning by doing. This is the deal that tests how well you have learned the methods in this book.

An extra profit will be in your new opinion of yourself. You will change from a doubter to a believer. Here you profit in a feeling of personal confidence.

You will note a new respect from other people. You have crossed the line from talker to doer. You are now a dealer in land, a creator of action. You have started on the road to your fortune in land.

EXPAND AND DEAL AGAIN

Using the experience gained from your first deal, move immediately to your second deal. Do not decide to sit back and enjoy the proceeds from your first deal.

Use your land dealing profits to buy more land to make more profits to buy more land to make more profits.

If you do this, you will in a few years have that much desired personal financial independence. You may even have a fortune.

USE YOUR EXPERIENCE

It is not necessary that each of your land deals be larger than its predecessor. In many cases they will be larger; however, that is not the main objective. Your objective is larger profits.

Experience will help you to be more efficient. Experience will help you obtain more land for your dollar, more improvements for your dollar, more sales for your dollar, and then more dollars for your land.

Consider less dollars spent for more dollars income, which means more dollars profit, and profit is the name of the game. Use your experience to increase your profits, then use those profits to obtain more land to again make more profits.

LARGER OPERATION—LARGER PROFIT

It is not always true that the larger the deal, the larger the profits. A large mistake can eliminate all the profit and even create a loss. We all remember Ford Motor Company's "Edsel." Do not let your desire to be a big time operator blind you to the dangers of too much too soon.

As you expand your land operation, keep your expenditures under strict control. Install an accounting system that will let you know your financial position at all times. Keep a cash reserve for the unexpected expenditure or expense.

Make your plans based on your financial condition, your knowledge, and your experience. When you know you are ready, then and only then move up to the big deal.

BIG DEAL—BIG PROFIT

Following the methods in this book will lead you to that time when you can make your big deal and your big profit.

The big deal with the big profit is no more difficult in many ways than the little deal—in fact, it may be easier. You now have experience, reputation, cash flow, and proven credit. You now have all the ingredients for a big success. Now is the time to act, and by your actions solidify your fortune.

YOU ARE THE EXPERT

When you reach this stage in your land dealing career you will have become the expert in dealing in land. You will know those things that allow you to make deals and profits that are only dreams to others.

BUY HARD

You are now able to deal from strength. You can look for and find those exceptional deals. You can play hard to get. You can drive the hard bargain in buying the land you want. Your experience, reputation and cash in hand will give you the power to buy to your best profit advantage.

SELL HARD

Because you have proven you can make money from land, you will now be approached by people wanting to do the same. These people will want to buy land from you with the hope that they in turn will make a profit.

You can now do the following:

1. Buy acreage that you feel can be resold in small tracts or lots at a profit.
2. Devise a plan or a number of plans for the profitable sale of these tracts or lots.
3. Explain one or more of these plans to one of the people who want to become a land dealer.
4. Sell all or part of your acreage along with the sales plan to the potential land dealer. You, of course, sell at a price that gives you a substantial profit.
5. You have used your experience, reputation, and knowledge

to help start someone on the road to being a successful land dealer. You have also made yourself a substantial profit.

MAKE A FORTUNE

First decide what you consider a fortune to be—decide how much you want to make and how much time and effort you are willing to expend to get it.

You pick the amount, then chart the course to reach your goal. Land can make you a little or a lot of money; land can make you rich. It is really up to you. Decide on the fortune you want, then go get it. The way, as always, is to start at the beginning. Study, research, decide, and do. Your first deal leads to the second, then the third, and then maybe to that big deal and that big profit.

You, the expert, buying, selling, and making more and more profits. These profits are the dollars that add up to your fortune.

YOU CAN DO IT!

Examples of ordinary people making money, enjoying life, and in some cases becoming rich from land are endless. If others can do it, then you can do it.

The one thing that stops most people from making their fortune in land is lack of belief in themselves. Believe you can do a thing and it is half done. Decide now to use this book as a guide to a more successful life. Decide now to convert your dreams into reality. Decide now to take action.

Your fortune in land may be just down your street, in your city, out in the country, at the lake, or you may be looking at it out your window. Wherever it is, find it. FIND YOUR LAND AND MAKE IT BRING YOU YOUR FORTUNE.

Index